COLLINS GEM

Slovene
PHRASE FINDER

GW00685395

HarperCollins*Publishers*

CONSULTANT
Andrea Albretti

OTHER GEM PHRASE FINDERS

DUTCH

FRENCH

GERMAN

GREEK

ITALIAN

PORTUGUESE

SPANISH

TURKISH

*Look out for Phrase Finder
Tape Packs!*

First published 1996
Copyright © HarperCollins Publishers
Reprint 10 9 8 7 6 5 4 3 2 1 0
Printed in Great Britain

ISBN 0 00-470883-0

Your *Collins Gem Phrase Finder* is designed to help you locate the exact phrase you need in any situation, whether for holiday or business. If you want to adapt the phrases, we have made sure that you can easily see where to substitute your own words (you can find them in the dictionary section), and the clear, alphabetical, two-colour layout gives you direct access to the different topics.

The *Phrase Finder* includes:

■ Over 70 topics arranged alphabetically from **ACCOMMODATION** to **WORK**. Each phrase is accompanied by a simple pronunciation guide which ensures that there's no problem over pronouncing the foreign words.

■ Practical hints and useful vocabulary highlighted in boxes. Where the English words appear first in the box, this indicates vocabulary you may need. Where the red Slovene words appear first, these are words you are more likely to see written on signs and notices.

WORDS APPEARING IN BLACK ARE ENGLISH WORDS	WORDS APPEARING IN RED ARE SLOVENE WORDS

■ Possible phrases you may hear in reply to your questions. The foreign phrases appear in red.

■ A clearly laid-out 5000-word dictionary: English words appear in black and Slovene words appear in red.

■ A basic grammar section which will enable you to build on your phrases.

It's worth spending time before you embark on your travels just looking through the topics to see what is covered and becoming familiar with what might be said to you.

Whatever the situation, your *Phrase Finder* is sure to help!

BUSINESS

- ACCOUNTS
- BUSINESS
- COMPUTERS
- FAX
- LETTERS
- OFFICE
- WORK

TRAVEL

- *see* **CAR**
- AIRPORT
- ARRIVAL
- BOAT & FERRY
- BUS
- CUSTOMS CONTROL
- TAXI
- TRAIN

EATING & DRINKING

- DRINKING
- EATING OUT
- VEGETARIAN
- WINES & SPIRITS

CAR

- BREAKDOWNS
- CAR–DRIVING
- CAR–HIRE
- CAR–PARTS
- PETROL STATION

DIFFICULTIES

- COMPLAINTS
- EMERGENCIES
- PROBLEMS

LEISURE

- CELEBRATIONS
- CINEMA
- ENTERTAINMENT
- HIKING
- MUSIC
- SIGHTSEEING & TOURIST OFFICE
- SKIING
- SPORT & LEISURE
- TELEVISION
- THEATRE

SHOPPING

- CLOTHES
- FOOD–GENERAL
- FOOD–FRUIT/VEGETABLES
- MAPS, GUIDES & NEWSPAPERS
- PHARMACY
- PHOTOS & VIDEOS
- POST OFFICE
- SHOPPING–SHOPS

ACCOMMODATION

- ACCOMMODATION
- CAMPING
- DISABLED TRAVELLERS
- HOTEL DESK
- PAYING
- ROOM SERVICE
- SIGHTSEEING & TOURIST OFFICE

PRACTICALITIES

- ALPHABET
- BASICS
- COLOUR & SHAPE
- DAYS, MONTHS & SEASONS
- DIRECTIONS
- LUGGAGE
- MEASUREMENTS & QUANTITIES
- MONEY
- NUMBERS
- PAYING
- QUESTIONS
- REPAIRS
- SIGNS & NOTICES
- TELEPHONE
- TIME–TIME PHRASES

HEALTH

- BODY
- DENTIST
- DOCTOR
- EMERGENCIES
- PHARMACY

MEETING PEOPLE

- BASICS
- CELEBRATIONS
- GREETINGS
- MAKING FRIENDS
- WEATHER
- WORK

CONTENTS

PRONOUNCING SLOVENE 6
GRAMMAR 101
DICTIONARY 111

LIST OF TOPICS

ACCOMMODATION
ACCOUNTS
AIRPORT
ALPHABET
ARRIVAL
BASICS
BOAT & FERRY
BODY
BREAKDOWNS
BUS
BUSINESS
CAMPING
CAR—DRIVING
CAR—HIRE
CAR—PARTS
CELEBRATIONS
CINEMA
CLOTHES
COLOUR & SHAPE
COMPLAINTS
COMPUTERS
CUSTOMS CONTROL
DAYS, MONTHS & SEASONS
DENTIST
DIRECTIONS
DISABLED TRAVELLERS
DOCTOR
DRINKING
EATING OUT
EMERGENCIES
ENTERTAINMENT
FAX
FOOD—GENERAL
FOOD—FRUIT
FOOD—VEGETABLES

GREETINGS
HIKING
HOTEL DESK
LETTERS
LUGGAGE
MAKING FRIENDS
MAPS, GUIDES & NEWSPAPERS
MEASUREMENTS & QUANTITIES
MONEY
MUSIC
NUMBERS
OFFICE
PAYING
PETROL STATION
PHARMACY
PHOTOS & VIDEOS
POST OFFICE
PROBLEMS
QUESTIONS
REPAIRS
ROOM SERVICE
SHOPPING—SHOPS
SIGHTSEEING & TOURIST OFFICE
SIGNS & NOTICES
SKIING
SPORT & LEISURE
TAXI
TELEPHONE
TELEVISION
THEATRE
TIME—TIME PHRASES
TRAIN
VEGETARIAN
WEATHER
WINES & SPIRITS
WORK

Slovene uses the same script as English. Mostly the letters have the same sound in all positions. Generally it is not difficult to pronounce, though there are one or two difficult sounds for English-speakers.

The following letters sound the same as in English: **b d f g h k l m n p s t v** *and* **z** *(though see below for* **l** *and* **v***). Slovene also has the letters* **š** *(like English 'sh'),* **č** *(like English 'ch') and* **ž** *(like 's' in 'pleasure'). Note that* **g** *is always hard as in 'lag', never soft as in 'large'.*

*The syllable to be stressed is marked in **heavy italics**.*

■ VOWELS

		PRONUNCIATION GUIDE
a	*pronounced as in f<u>a</u>r*	*a*
e	*pronounced as in p<u>e</u>t*	*e*
	in some words, as in pol<u>i</u>ce	*ee*
i	*pronounced as in pol<u>i</u>ce*	*ee*
o	*pronounced as in n<u>o</u>t*	*o*
u	*pronounced as in bl<u>u</u>e*	*oo*

■ DIFFICULT SOUNDS

c   *is pronounced like the 'ts' in 'tsar'.*

h   *is pronounced in all positions, even at the end of words, where we insert a hyphen to keep it separate from the vowel eg:* **lahko** *la-**hko**,* **hvala** *hva-la,* **kruh** *kroo-h.*

j   *is always pronounced like 'y' in 'yes', even where it occurs after a consonant or at the end of a syllable or word, which we show using superscript* ʸ, *eg:* **gleženj** *gle-zhenʸ,* **manj** *manʸ,* **dvoposteljno** *dvo-pos-telʸ-no.*

l & v *are pronounced like w before consonants and at the end of words. We have represented this by superscript* ʷ, *eg:* **volk** *voʷk,* **videl** *vee-deʷ,* **avto** *aʷ-to,* **lev** *leʷ.*

r   *is rolled; it can be a syllable in its own right (shown as rr), eg:* **prho** *prr-ho,* **vrv** *vrrv.*

If you haven't booked accommodation in advance, go to the local tourist office. It should not be difficult to get a room in a hotel unless there is an international event taking place or if you are heading to a popular tourist area in high season (particularly July and August). Private houses also rent out rooms **sobe** *and a popular option is 'farm tourism' where you can stay in pleasant rural surroundings.*

ROOMS	SOBE
GUESTHOUSE	PENZION
FULL	ZASEDENO

Do you have a list of accommodation with prices?
Imate seznam prenočišč s cenami?
ee-**ma**-te sez-**nam** pre-no-**cheeshch** s **tse**-na-mee

Is there a hotel near here?
Je tukaj blizu kakšen hotel?
ye **too**-kaʸ **blee**-zu **kak**-shen ho-**tel**

We'd like to stay on a farm
Radi bi šli na kmetijo
ra-dee bee shlee na kme-**tee**-yo

Have you any vacancies?
Imate proste sobe?
ee-**ma**-te **pro**-ste **so**-be

I'd like a room...
Rad(a) bi sobo...
rad(a) bee **so**-bo...

single	**double**
enoposteljno	dvoposteljno
e-no-pos-telʸ-no	**dvo**-pos-telʸ-no

with bath	**with shower**	**with a double bed**
s kopalnico	s prho	z zakonsko posteljo
s ko-**pal**-nee-tso	s **prr**-ho	z za-**kon**-sko **pos**-tel-yo

CONT...

with two beds
z dvema posteljama
z **dve**-ma **pos**-tel-ya-ma

with an extra bed for a child
z dodatno posteljo za otroka
z do-**dat**-no **pos**-tel-yo za o-**tro**-ka

We'd like two rooms...
Radi bi dve sobi...
ra-dee bee dve **so**-bee...

next to each other
eno zraven druge
e-no **zra**-ven **droo**-ge

We want to stay ...
Ostali bomo...
os-**ta**-lee bo-mo...

1 night
eno noč
e-no noch

2 nights
dve noči
dve no-**chee**

from...till...
od...do...
od...do...

How much is a room...?
Koliko stane soba...?
ko-lee-ko **sta**-ne **so**-ba...

with full board
s popolno oskrbo
s po-**pow**-no os-**krr**-bo

Is breakfast included?
Je zajtrk vključen?
ye **zay**-trrk v-**klyoo**-chen

Is there a reduction for children?
Je za otroke popust?
ye za o-**tro**-ke po-**poost**

Have you anything cheaper?
Imate kaj cenejšega?
ee-**ma**-te ka^y tse-**ney**-sheg-a

Is there another hotel here?
Je v tem kraju še kakšen hotel?
ye oo tem **kra**-yoo she **kak**-shen ho-**tel**

■ YOU MAY HEAR

Ste rezervirali sobo?
 *ste re-zer-**vee**-ra-lee **so**-bo*
 Have you booked a room?

Trenutno so vse sobe zasedene
 *tre-**noot**-no so ᵂse **so**-be za-**se**-de-ne*
 We are full at present

Kako dolgo nameravate ostati?
 *ka-**ko doᵂ**-go na-me-**ra**-va-te o-**sta**-tee*
 How long do you intend to stay?

Bi mi prosim povedali svoje ime?
 *bee mee pro-seem po-**ve**-da-lee **svo**-ye ee-**me***
 May I have your name, please

Tukaj se podpišite, prosim
 ***too**-kaʸ se pod-**pee**-shee-te pro-seem*
 Please sign here

■ YOU MAY SEE

*If you take a room you may be asked to fill in a registration form.
You may have to fill in similar forms when renting a car, etc.*

Ime...	**Name...**
Priimek...	**Surname...**
Državljanstvo...	**Nationality...**
Stalno prebivališče	**Address...**
Datum rojstva...	**Date of Birth...**
Številka potnega lista	**Passport Number...**
Datum...	**Date...**
Podpis...	**Signature...**

■ HOTEL DESK ■ CAMPING ■ ROOM SERVICE

ACCOUNT	RAČUN / FAKTURA
ACCOUNTANT m/f	RAČUNOVODJA / RAČUNOVODKINJA
ACCOUNTS DEPARTMENT	RAČUNOVODSTVO

I'd like to speak to someone in accounts (man speaking)
Rad bi govoril z nekom v računovodstvu
rad bee go-vo-ree^w z ne-kom oo ra-choo-no-vod-stvoo

I'd like to speak to someone in accounts (woman speaking)
Rada bi govorila z nekom v računovodstvu
ra-da bee go-vo-ree-la z ne-kom oo ra-choo-no-vod-stvoo

It's regarding invoice number...
Gre za račun številka...
gre za ra-choon shte-veel-ka...

Please could you settle this account
Bi prosim poravnali ta račun
bee pro-seem po-rav-na-lee ta ra-choon

We are still waiting for the invoice to be settled
Še zmeraj čakamo na plačilo računa
she zme-ra^y cha-ka-mo na pla-chee-lo ra-choo-na

Please send the invoice to...
Prosim pošljite račun na...
pro-seem posh-lyee-te ra-choon na...

■ **YOU MAY HEAR**

Ta račun je bil plačan
ta ra-choon ye bee^w pla-chan
This paymant was made

Računovodja trenutno ni v pisarni
ra-choo-no-vod-ya tre-noot-no nee oo pee-sar-nee
The accountant isn't in the office at the moment

■ **BUSINESS** ■ **NUMBERS** ■ **TELEPHONE**

The main airport in Brnik is 25 km from the centre of Ljubljana. There is a regular bus service to and from the airport. Most signs will be in English and you may not need to speak any Slovene at the airport.

AIRPORT	**LETALIŠČE**
DEPARTURE	**ODHOD**
ARRIVAL	**PRIHOD**
DELAY	**ZAMUDA**
INTERNATIONAL FLIGHTS	**MEDNARODNI POLETI**
NATIONAL/DOMESTIC FLIGHTS	**DOMAČI POLETI**
FLIGHT	**POLET**
BAGGAGE RECLAIM	**PRTLJAGA**
CUSTOMS	**CARINA**
INFORMATION DESK	**INFORMACIJE**
EXIT *(departure gate)*	**IZHOD**

Where is the luggage for the flight from...?
Kje je prtljaga poleta iz...?
k^ye ye prrt-**lya**-ga po-**le**-ta eez...

To the airport, please
Na letališče, prosim
na le-ta-**leesh**-che pro-seem

How much is it to the airport?
Koliko stane do letališča?
ko-lee-ko **sta**-ne do le-ta-**leesh**-cha

How do I get to...?
Kako pridem v...
ka-**ko** pree-dem oo...

this town
to mesto
to **mes**-to

this village
to vas
to vas

Which is the bus for the town centre?
Kateri avtobus pelje v središče mesta?
ka-**tee**-ree a^w-to-boos **pel**-ye oo sre-**deesh**-che **mes**-ta

Where is the taxi rank?
Kje je postajališče taksijev?
k^ye ye po-sta-ya-**leesh**-che **tak**-see-ye^w

■ARRIVAL ■BÜS ■LUGGAGE ■TAXI

X,Y,Q,W are not native to the Slovene language. You will, however, see these letters in imported words. The sounds of the 25 letters of the Slovene alphabet are given below. See **PRONOUNCING SLOVENE** *for the sounds of different letter combinations:*

	SOUND	AS IN
A	a	**far**
B	b	**balloon**
C	ts	**tsar**
Č	ch	**church**
D	d	**dad**
E	e	**exit**
F	f	**fur**
G	g	**get**
H	h	**home**
I	ee	**police**
J	y	**yes**
K	k	**kite**
L	l	**late**
M	m	**milk**
N	n	**no**
O	o	**port**
P	p	**peace**
R	r	**red** (slightly rolled)
S	s	**son**
Š	sh	**ship**
T	t	**top**
U	oo	**blue**
V	v	**vet**
Z	z	**zebra**
Ž	zh	**pleasure**

■ PRONOUNCING SLOVENE

Slovenia has over 60 border crossings with Italy, Austria, Hungary and Croatia. Most of them are very small but they are all open 24 hours.

STATE BORDER	**DRŽAVNA MEJA**
CHECKPOINT	**MEJNI PREHOD**

Here is...
Izvolite...
ee-**zvo**-lee-te...

my passport
moj potni list
moy **pot**-nee leest

my identity card
mojo osebno izkaznico
mo-yo o-**seb**-no eez-**kaz**-nee-tso

my driving licence
moje vozniško dovoljenje
mo-ye voz-**neesh**-ko do-vol-**yen**-ye

I'm travelling...
Potujem...
po-**too**-yem...

as a tourist
kot turist
kot too-**reest**

on business
poslovno
po-**slov**-no

I'm staying...
Ostanem...
o-**sta**-nem...

one week
en teden
en **te**-den

one month
en mesec
en **mes**-ets

Do you have a road map of Slovenia?
Imate cestno karto Slovenije?
ee-**ma**-te **tsest**-no **kar**-to slo-**ve**-nee-ye

■ YOU MAY HEAR

Potni list, prosim
pot-nee leest pro-seem
Your passport, please

Imate kaj za prijaviti?
ee-**ma**-te ka^y za pree-**ya**-vee-tee
Do you have anything to declare?

■ BUS ■ MONEY ■ TRAIN

Yes
Ja *or* Da
yȧ   da

No
Ne
ne

Please
Prosim
pro-seem

Thank you
Hvala
***hva*-la**

Thank you very much
Najlepša hvala
*na**ʸ**-lep-sha **hva**-la*

Good day (hello)
Dober dan
***do*-ber dan**

Goodbye
Na svidenje
*na **svee**-den-ye*

Don't mention it
Prosim *or* Ni za kaj
*pro-seem   nee za ka**ʸ***

Pardon?
Prosim?
pro-seem

Excuse me!
Oprostite!
*o-pro-**stee**-te*

I'm sorry
Žal mi je
*zha**ʷ** mee ye*

Mr
gospod
*go-**spod***

Mrs/Ms
gospa
*go-**spa***

Miss
gospodična
*go-spo-**deech**-na*

Where?
Kje?
kʸe

Where is...?
Kje je...?
kʸe ye...

Where are...?
Kje so...?
kʸe so...

Where are the toilets?
Kje so toaletni prostori?
*kʸe so to-a-**let**-nee pro-**sto**-ree*

I'd like...
Želim...
*zhe-**leem**...*

We'd like...
Želimo...
*zhe-**lee**-mo...*

this
to
to

that
tisto
***tee**-sto*

14

Do you have...?
Imate...?
ee-**ma**-te...

How much is it?
Koliko stane?
ko-lee-ko **sta**-ne

How much are they?
Koliko stanejo?
ko-lee-ko **sta**-ne-yo

When is...?
Kdaj je...?
kda^y ye...

I don't understand
Ne razumem
ne ra-**zoo**-mem

Please write it down
Napišite mi, prosim
na-**pee**-shee-te mee pro-seem

Do you speak English?
Govorite angleško?
go-vo-**ree**-te an-**glesh**-ko

How do you say this in Slovene?
Kako se to reče po slovensko?
ka-**ko** se to re-che po slo-**ven**-sko

What does this mean?
Kaj to pomeni?
ka^y to po-**me**-nee

Please help me!
Pomagajte mi, prosim!
po-**ma**-ga^y-te mee pro-seem

■ GREETINGS ■ NUMBERS ■ ASKING QUESTIONS

*From April to September a boat sails daily from **Portorož** to Venice returning in the evening. The journey takes about 2 hours. There is also a hydrofoil service.*

POLETNI VOZNI RED	SUMMER TIMETABLE

When is the next ship to...?
Kdaj odpluje naslednja ladja v...?
kda^y od-**ploo**-ye nas-**led**-nya **la**-dya oo...

When is the next hydrofoil to...?
Kdaj odpluje naslednji gliser v...?
kda^y od-**ploo**-ye nas-**led**-nyee **glee**-ser oo...

How much is...?
Koliko stane...?
ko-lee-ko **sta**-ne...

a single ticket
enosmerna vozovnica
e-no-smer-na vo-**zo^w**-nee-tsa

a return ticket
povratna vozovnica
po^w-**rat**-na vo-**zo^w**-nee-tsa

2 tickets...
dve vozovnici...
dve vo-**zo^w**-nee-tsee...

for adults
za odrasle
za od-**ra**-sle

for children
za otroke
za ot-**ro**-ke

How long does it take?
Kako dolgo traja vožnja?
ka-**ko** do^w-go **tra**-ya **vozh**-nya

Where does the ship leave from?
Od kod odpluje ladja?
od kod od-**ploo**-ye **la**-dya

What time is...?
Ob kateri uri je...?
ob ka-**tee**-ree **oo**-ree ye...

the first ship
prva ladja
prr-va **la**-dya

the last ship
zadnja ladja
zad-nya **la**-dya

Have you a timetable?
Imate vozni red?
ee-**ma**-te **voz**-nee red

My ... hurts
... me boli
... me bo-**lee**

arm	roka	**ro**-ka
back	hrbet / križ	**hrr**-bet / kreezh
bone	kost	kost
ear	uho	**oo**-ho
eye	oko	**o**-ko
finger	prst	prrst
foot	noga	**no**-ga
hand	roka	**ro**-ka
head	glava	**gla**-va
heart	srce	**srr**-tse
hip	bok	bok
joint	sklep	sklep
kidney	ledvica	led-**vee**-tsa
knee	koleno	ko-**le**-no
leg	noga	**no**-ga
liver	jetra	**ye**-tra
mouth	usta	**oo**-sta
muscle	mišica	**mee**-shee-tsa
neck	vrat	vrat
nose	nos	nos
shoulder	rama	**ra**-ma
stomach / tummy	želodec / trebuh	zhe-**lo**-dets / **tre**-boo-h
throat	grlo	**grr**-lo
thumb	palec	**pa**-lets
toe	prst na nogi	prrst na **no**-gee
wrist	zapestje	za-**pest**-ye

■ DOCTOR ■ EMERGENCIES ■ PHARMACY

If you breakdown, contact **AMZS** *(the Slovene Automobile Association). Their emergency number is* **987**.

Can you help me?
Mi lahko pomagate?
mee la-**hko** po-**ma**-ga-te

My car has broken down
Avto se mi je pokvaril
a**w**-to se mee ye po-**kva**-ree**w**

I've run out of petrol
Zmanjkalo mi je bencina
zmany-ka-lo mee ye ben-**tsee**-na

I have a flat tyre
Imam prazno gumo
ee-**mam praz**-no **goo**-mo

Can you give me a push please
Me lahko porinete, prosim
me la-**hko** po-**ree**-ne-te pro-seem

The battery is flat
Baterija je prazna
ba-te-**ree**-ya ye **pra**-zna

Where is the nearest car service?
Kje je najbližji avtomobilski servis?
k^ye ye na^y-**bleezh**-yee a^w-to-mo-**beel**-skee **ser**-vees

Do you have spare parts for...*(give make of car)*
Imate rezervne dele za...
ee-**ma**-te re-**zerv**-ne de-le za...

There is something wrong with the...
Nekaj je narobe z...
ne-ka^y ye na-**ro**-be z...

How long will the repairs take?
Kako dolgo bo trajalo popravilo?
ka-**ko** do**w**-go bo **tra**-ya-lo po-pra-**vee**-lo

■CAR – PARTS ■REPAIRS

In larger towns, tokens are used on the bus, otherwise you have to have the exact fare. You can buy tokens from kiosks and bars. For long distance travel, tickets can be bought on the bus.

TOKEN FOR A CITY BUS	ŽETON ZA AVTOBUS
TICKET	VOZOVNICA

Do you sell bus tokens?
Ali prodajate žetone za avtobus?
a-lee pro-**da**-ya-te zhe-**to**-ne za a**ʷ**-to-boos

10 tokens, please
deset žetonov, prosim
de-**set** zhe-**to**-noʷ pro-seem

Is there a bus to...?
Ali vozi avtobus v...?
a-lee **vo**-zee a**ʷ**-to-boos oo...

Which bus goes to...?
Kateri avtobus pelje v...?
ka-**tee**-ree a**ʷ**-to-boos **pel**-ye oo...

I'm / We're going to...
Grem / Gremo v...
grem / **gre**-mo oo...

Where is the bus stop?
Kje je avtobusna postaja?
k**ʸ**e ye a**ʷ**-to-boos-na po-**sta**-ya

How much is a ticket?
Koliko stane vozovnica?
ko-lee-ko **sta**-ne vo-**zo**-nee-tsa

to the centre
do center
do **tsen**-ter

to this village
do te vasi
do te va-**see**

How often are the buses to...?
Kako pogosto vozijo avtobusi v...?
ka-**ko** po-**go**-sto vo-zee-yo a**ʷ**-to-boo-see oo...

When is...?
Kdaj pelje...?
kda**ʸ** **pel**-ye...

the first
prvi
prr-vee

the last
zadnji
zad-nyee

bus to...
avtobus v...
a**ʷ**-to-boos oo...

Please tell me when to get off
Povejte mi prosim, kdaj naj izstopim
po-**vey**-te mee pro-seem kda**ʸ** na**ʸ** eez-**sto**-peem

◼ YOU MAY HEAR

To je vaša postaja
to ye **va**-sha po-**sta**-ya
This is your stop

Morali boste prestopiti v...
mo-ra-lee **bo**-ste pres-**to**-pee-tee oo...
You have to change at...

◼ TAXI

19

HEAD OFFICE	SEDEŽ PODJETJA
REPRESENTATIVE OFFICE	PREDSTAVNIŠTVO
FIRM	FIRMA / PODJETJE
MANAGING DIRECTOR m/f	GENERALNI DIREKTOR / DIREKTORICA
MEETING	SESTANEK
TO SIGN A CONTRACT	PODPISATI POGODBO
CONFERENCE	KONFERENCA / SEJA
TRADE FAIR	SEJEM

Where is the ... company?
Kje je firma...?
*kʸe ye **feer**-ma...*

Where is your head office?
Kje je sedež vašega podjetja?
*kʸe ye **se**-dezh va-sheg-a pod-**yet**-ya*

Do you have a representative office in England?
Imate predstavništvo v Angliji?
*ee-**ma**-te pred-**sta**ʷ-neesht-vo oo **An**-glee-yee*

What is the address?
Kakšen je naslov?
***kak**-shen ye na-**slo**ʷ*

Our address is...
Naš naslov je...
*nash na-**slo**ʷ ye...*

Please send me your annual report
Pošljite mi prosim vaše letno poročilo
***posh**-lyee-te mee pro-seem **va**-she **let**-no po-ro-**chee**-lo*

Do you have a card?
Imate vizitko?
*ee-**ma**-te vee-**zeet**-ko*

Here's my card
Izvolite mojo vizitko
*eez-**vo**-lee-te **mo**-yo vee-**zeet**-ko*

I'd like to see the director
Rad(a) bi k direktorju
*rad(a) bee k dee-**rek**-tor-yoo*

I have an appointment with...
Dogovorjen(a) sem z...
*do-go-vor-**yen**(a) sem z...*

a ... o'clock
ob ...
ob ...

I'm sorry I'm late *(man)*
Oprostite, pozen sem
*o-pro-**stee**-te **po**-zen sem*

(woman)
Oprostite, pozna sem
*o-pro-**stee**-te **po**-zna sem*

I'd like to meet... *(man)*
Rad bi se sestal z...
*rad bee se se-**sta**W z...*

(woman)
Rada bi se sestala z...
***ra**-da bee se se-**sta**-la z...*

I'm staying at the hotel...
Sem v hotelu...
*sem oo ho-**te**-loo...*

■ YOU MAY HEAR

Ste dogovorjeni?
*ste do-go-vor-**ye**-nee*
Do you have an appointment?

Sedite in počakajte trenutek prosim
***se**-dee-te een po-**cha**-kaY-te tre-**noo**-tek pro-seem*
Please take a seat and wait a minute

Takoj bo prišel
*ta-**koy** bo **pree**-shel*
He'll be here in 2 minutes

Takoj bo prišla
*ta-**koy** bo **preesh**-la*
She'll be here in 2 minutes

Gospoda... / Gospe... danes ni v pisarni
*gos-**po**-da... / gos-**pe**... **da**-nes nee oo pee-**sar**-nee*
Mr... / Ms... is not in the office today

■ FAX ■ LETTERS ■ OFFICE ■ TELEPHONE

Slovenia is dotted with well-equipped campsites which are graded according to the amenities and services they offer. If you are planning your camping in advance, check before that the camp is open as some close during the winter months.

CAMPSITE	KAMP
CAR-CAMP	AVTOKAMP
DRINKING WATER	PITNA VODA
RUBBISH	SMETI / ODPADKI

Do you have a list of campsites with prices?
Imate seznam kampov s cenami?
ee-**ma**-te sez-**nam** kam-po^W s **tse**-na-mee

Can we camp here?
Lahko tukaj kampiramo?
la-**hko** too-kaÿ kam-**pee**-ramo

We'd like to stay for ... days
Radi bi ostali ... dni
ra-dee bee o-**sta**-lee ... dnee

How much is it...?	per day	per week	per person
Koliko stane...?	na dan	na teden	na osebo
ko-lee-ko **sta**-ne...	na dan	na **ted**-en	na o-**se**-bo

How much is it...?	for a tent	for a caravan	for a car
Koliko stane...?	za šotor	za prikolico	za avto
ko-lee-ko **sta**-ne...	za **sho**-tor	za pree-**ko**-lee-tso	za a^W-to

Where is...?	the reception	the drinking water
Kje je...?	recepcija	pitna voda
kÿe ye...	re-**tsep**-tsee-ya	**peet**-na **vod**-a

Where are...?	the toilets	the showers
Kje so...?	toaletni prostori	tuši
kÿe so...	to-a-**let**-nee pro-**sto**-ree	**too**-shee

Where can we park the car?
Kje lahko parkiramo avto?
kÿe la-**hko** par-**kee**-ra-mo a^W-to

■SIGHTSEEING & TOURIST OFFICE

*Traffic signs are reasonably good in Slovenia and there are plenty of rest areas and inns on the roads. If you are driving in the winter, snow can take you by surprise, so make sure you have the necessary winter equipment for the car. The speed limit is 60 kph in built-up areas, 80 kph on other roads and 120 kph on motorways. There is a motorway toll **CESTNINA** .*
There are car parks in all larger towns and a fee is charged (usually) per hour. An efficient tow-away operation is run in larger towns to remove illegally parked vehicles.
International car insurance is required for all foreign vehicles. Green Card forms are available at all border crossings.

AVTOCESTA	MOTORWAY
CENTER	CITY CENTRE
CESTNINA	TOLL
ENOSMERNA CESTA	ONE WAY ROAD
GOSTILNA OB CESTI	ROADSIDE INN
NEVARNOST	DANGER
SREDIŠČE MESTA	CITY CENTRE
STOJ	STOP
VOZI POČASI	DRIVE SLOWLY
VOZITE PO LEVI \ DESNI	KEEP TO THE LEFT \ RIGHT
ZASEBNA CESTA	PRIVATE ROAD

Which road goes to...?
Katera cesta vodi v...?
ka-**tee**-ra **tses**-ta **vod**-ee oo...

We're going to...
Gremo v...
grem-o oo...

Can I park here?
Lahko tukaj parkiram?
la-**hko** too-kaʸ par-**kee**-ram

Do we need snow chains?
Ali potrebujemo snežne verige?
a-lee po-tre-**boo**-ye-mo snezh-ne ver-**ee**-ge

■ **BREAKDOWNS** ■ **CAR–HIRE / PARTS** ■ **PETROL STATION**

Many of the big international car hire firms have offices in Slovenia. You find them in larger towns, tourist resorts and at airports. Tourist offices should be able to arrange renting a car for you. The driver hiring a car must be over 21 (in some places over 18) and have held a driving licence for at least 2 years (in some places 1 year). The basic rate is exclusive of fuel, road tolls, parking fees, comprehensive insurance and tax.

DRIVING LICENCE	VOZNIŠKO DOVOLJENJE
FULLY COMPREHENSIVE INSURANCE	POLNO KASKO ZAVAROVANJE

I'd like to hire a car *(man)*   *(woman)*
  Rad bi najel avto   Rada bi najela avto
  rad bee na-ye^w a^w-to   ***ra**-da bee na-**ye**-la a^w-to*

a small car	**a large car**
majhen avto	velik avto
ma^y-hen a^w-to	*ve-leek a^w-to*

Do you have an automatic car?
  Imate avto z avtomatskimi prestavami?
  *ee-**ma**-te a^w-to z-a^w-to-**mat**-skee-mee pre-**sta**-va-mee*

What is the rate...?	**per day**	**per week**
Kakšna je cena...?	na dan	na teden
***kak**-shna je **tsen**-a...*	*na dan*	*na **ted**-en*

I also want insurance	**Is there a deposit?**
Rad(a) bi tudi zavarovanje	Je treba plačati depozit?
*rad(a) bee **too**-dee za-va-ro-**van**-ye*	*je **tre**-ba **pla**-cha-tee de-po-**zeet***

Where do I return the car?
  Kje moram vrniti avto?
  *k^{y}e **mo**-ram **vrr**-nee-tee a^w-to*

■ YOU MAY HEAR

Bencinski tank mora biti ob vrnitvi poln
  *ben-**tseen**-skee tank **mo**-ra **bee**-tee ob vrr-**neet**-vee po^{w}n*
The tank should be full on return

The ... doesn't work	The ... don't work
...ne deluje	...ne delujejo
...ne de-**loo**-ye	...ne de-**loo**-ye-yo

accelerator pospeševalec *pos-pe-she-**va**-lets*

alternator dinamo na izmenični tok *dee-**na**-mo na eez-**me**-neech-nee tok*

battery baterija *ba-te-**ree**-ya*

bonnet pokrov *pok-ro**w***

brakes zavora *za-**vo**-ra*

choke dušilka *doo-**sheel**-ka*

clutch sklopka *sklop-ka*

distributor regulator *re-goo-**la**-tor*

engine motor *mo-**tor***

exhaust izpušna cev *ees-**poosh**-na tsev*

fuse varovalka *va-ro-**val**-ka*

gears prestava *pres-**ta**-va*

handbrake ročna zavora *roch-na za-**vo**-ra*

headlights prednja luč *pred-nya looch*

indicator smerno kazalo *smer-no ka-**za**-lo*

pointer kazalec *ka-**za**-lets*

radiator grelec *gre-lets*

reverse gear vzvratna prestava *w zvrat-na pre-**sta**-va*

seat belt varnostni pas *var-nost-nee pas*

spark plug svečka *svech-ka*

steering krmilne naprave *krr-**meel**-ne na-**pra**-ve*

steering wheel volan *vo-**lan***

tyre guma *goo-ma*

wheel kolo *ko-**lo***

windscreen vetrobransko steklo *vet-ro-**bran**-sko **ste**-klo*

■ **BREAKDOWNS** ■ **PETROL STATION**

Happy Birthday
Vse najboljše za rojstni dan
^wse naY-**bol**Y-she za royst-nee dan

Happy Anniversary
Prijetno obletnico
pree-**yet**-no o-**blet**-nee-tso

Merry Christmas
Vesel božič
ves-e^w **bo**-zheech

Happy New Year
Srečno novo leto
srech-no **no**-vo **le**-to

Happy Easter
Prijetne velikonočne praznike
pree-**yet**-ne vel-ee-ko-**noch**-ne **praz**-nee-ke

Have a good trip
Srečno pot
srech-no pot

Have a good holiday
Prijeten dopust
pree-**yet**-en do-**poost**

Welcome
Dobrodošli
do-bro-**dosh**-lee

Enjoy your meal
Dober tek
do-ber **tek**

Thanks, and the same to you
Hvala enako
hva-la e-**na**-ko

Cheers
Na zdravje
na **zdrav**-ye

Congratulations
Iskrene čestitke
ees-**kre**-ne ches-**teet**-ke

■ LETTERS ■ MAKING FRIENDS

*In Slovenia, films are not dubbed. The titles of the films,
however, are translated (sometimes beyond recognition).*

CINEMA	KINO

Where is the cinema?
Kje je kino?
*kYe ye **kee**-no*

What's on at the cinema...? *(give name of cinema)*
Kaj igra v kinu...?
*kaY ee-**gra** oo **kee**-noo*

What time does the film start?
Kdaj se začne film?
*kdaY se zach-**ne** feelm*

What time does the film end?
Ob kateri uri konča film?
*ob ka-**tee**-ree **oo**-ree kon-**cha** feelm*

How much are the tickets?
Koliko stane karta?
*ko-lee-ko **sta**-ne **kar**-ta*

2 tickets for the showing at... *(give time of performance)*
Dve karti za predstavo ob...
*dve **kar**-tee za pred-**sta**-vo ob...*

■ YOU MAY HEAR

Žal mi je, karte so razprodane
*zhaW mee ye **kar**-te so raz-pro-**da**-ne*
I'm sorry, we're sold out

Lahko vidim vašo karto, prosim
*la-**hko** vee-deem **va**-sho **kar**-to pro-seem*
May I see your ticket, please?

■ ENTERTAINMENT   ■ TELEVISION

The word for size for clothes and shoes is **številka**

women

sizes	
UK	EC
10	36
12	38
14	40
16	42
18	44
20	46

men - suits

sizes	
UK	EC
36	46
38	48
40	50
42	52
44	54
46	56

shoes

sizes			
UK	EC	UK	EC
2	35	8	42
3	36	9	43
4	37	10	44
5	38	11	45
6	39		
7	41		

May I try this on?
Lahko to pomerim?
la-**hko** to po-**me**-reem

Do you have a size...?
Imate številko...?
ee-**ma**-te shte-**veel**-ko...

It's too small for me
Premajhno mi je
pre-**may**-hne mee ye

Where is the fitting room?
Kje je kabina za preoblačenje?
k^ye ye ka-**bee**-na za pre-o-**bla**-chen-ye

smaller	bigger
manjšo	večjo
man^y-sho	**vech**-yo

It's too big for me
Preveliko mi je
pre-ve-**lee**-ko mee ye

■ **YOU MAY HEAR**

Katero številko želite?
Ka-**tee**-ro shte-**veel**-ko zhe-**lee**-te
What size do you take?

Pomerite!
po-**me**-ree-te
Try it on!

Ali se vam prilega?
a-lee se vam pree-**le**-ga
Does it fit you?

■ **NUMBERS** ■ **PAYING** ■ **SHOPPING**

COTTON	BOMBAŽ	SILK	SVILA
LEATHER	USNJE	WOOL	VOLNA

belt	pas	*pas*
blouse	bluza	*bloo-za*
bra	nedrček	*ne-drr-chek*
coat	plašč	*plashch*
dress	obleka	*o-ble-ka*
fur coat	krzneni plašč	*krrz-ne-nee plashch*
gloves	rokavice	*ro-ka-vee-tse*
hat	klobuk	*klo-book*
jacket	jopič / suknjič	*yo-peech / sook-nyeech*
jumper	pulover	*poo-lo-ver*
knickers	spodnje hlače	*spod-nʸe hla-che*
nightdress	spalna srajca	*spal-na sraʸ-tsa*
pyjamas	pižama	*pee-zha-ma*
raincoat	dežni plašč	*dezh-nee plashch*
sandals	sandali	*san-da-lee*
scarf	ruta	*roo-ta*
shawl	šal	*shal*
shirt	srajca	*sraʸ-tsa*
shorts	kratke hlače	*krat-ke hla-che*
skirt	krilo	*kree-lo*
socks	kratke nogavice	*krat-ke no-ga-vee-tse*
suit	obleka	*o-ble-ka*
swimsuit	kopalna obleka	*ko-pal-na o-ble-ka*
tie	kravata	*kra-va-ta*
t-shirt	majica	*ma-yee-tsa*
track suit	trenirka	*tre-neer-ka*
trousers	hlače	*hla-che*
underwear	spodnje perilo	*spod-nʸe pe-ree-lo*
vest	majica	*ma-yee-tsa*

Key words for describing colours in Slovene are:

svetlo	**light**	temno	**dark**
black	črn		chrn
blue	moder		**mo**-der
brown	rjav		rya^w
gold	zlat		zlat
green	zelen		ze-**len**
grey	siv		see^w
orange	oranžen		o-**ran**-zhen
purple	škrlaten		shkrr-**la**-ten
red	rdeč		rr-**dech**
silver	srebrn		srre-**brrn**
white	bel		be^w
yellow	rumen		roo-**men**

■ SHAPE

big	velik	**ve**-leek
fat	debel	de-**be**^w
flat	raven	**ra**-ven
large	velik	**ve**-leek ,
long	dolg	do^wg
narrow	ozek	**o**-zek
round	okrogel	o-**krog**-e^w
small	majhen	**ma**^y-hen
tall	visok	vee-**sok**
thick	debel	de-**be**^w
thin	vitek	**vee**-tek
tiny	majcen	**ma**^y-tsen
wide	širok	shee-**rok**

*Note: all colours and shapes are adjectives and are given in their masculine form (See **GRAMMAR**).*

The ... does not work
...ne deluje.
*...ne de-**loo**-ye*

The ... do not work
...ne delujejo.
*...ne de-**loo**-ye-yo*

shower
prha
***prr**-ha*

telephone
telefon
*te-le-**fon***

heating
gretje
***gret**-ye*

light
luč
looch

water tap
vodna pipa
***vod**-na **pee**-pa*

air conditioning
klimatska naprava
*klee-**mat**-ska na-**pra**-va*

The window won't open
Okno se ne da odpreti
***o**-kno se ne da od-**pre**-tee*

The window won't close
Okno se ne da zapreti
***o**-kno se ne da za-**pre**-tee*

I don't like the room
Soba mi ni všeč
***so**-ba mee nee ᵂshech*

It's noisy (room)
Hrupna je
***hroop**-na ye*

It's too small (room)
Premajhna je
*pre-**maʸ**-hna ye*

It's too hot (room)
Prevroča je
*prev-**ro**-cha ye*

It's too cold (room)
Premrzla je
*pre-**mrr**-zla ye*

It's broken
Pokvarjeno je
*pok-**var**-ye-no ye*

Who is in charge of complaints?
Kdo je odgovoren za reklamacije?
*kdo ye od-go-**vo**-ren za rek-la-**ma**-tsee-ye*

I didn't order this (man)
Tega nisem naročil
*te-ga **nee**-sem na-**ro**-cheeᵂ*

(woman)
Tega nisem naročila
*te-ga **nee**-sem na-**ro**-chee-la*

■ **PROBLEMS** ■ **REPAIRS** ■ **ROOM SERVICE**

Most of the words in computer terminology are either the same, or sound the same as English but are spelt in the Slovene way. At any rate, you will be understood using the English words.

COMPUTER	RAČUNALNIK
PC	OSEBNI RAČUNALNIK
FLOPPY DISK	GIBKI DISK
HARD DISK	TRDI DISK
PRINTER	TISKALNIK
PROGRAMME	PROGRAM

What computer do you use?
Kateri računalnik uporabljate?
ka-**tee**-ree ra-choo-**nal**-neek oo-po-**rab**-lya-te

Is it IBM compatible?
Ali je IBM kompatibilen?
a-lee ye ee-be-em kom-pa-tee-**bee**-len

What programme do you use?
Kateri program uporabljate?
ka-**tee**-ree pro-**gram** oo-po-**rab**-lya-te

Which version do you have?
Katero verzijo imate?
ka-**tee**-ro **ver**-zee-yo ee-**ma**-te

Do you have E-mail?
Imate elektronsko pošto?
ee-**ma**-te e-lek-**tron**-sko **posh**-to

What is your address?
Vaš naslov, prosim?
vash na-**slo**ʷ **pro**-seem

■ OFFICE ■ WORK

*Personal luggage and items intended for personal use can be brought into Slovenia without customs duties. For items you are unsure about check with the **National Customs Administration as to whether duty is required**. At the larger border crossings there are duty-free shops.*

MEJNI PREHOD	**CHECKPOINT**
KONTROLA POTNIH LISTOV	**PASSPORT CONTROL**
CARINSKA DEKLARACIJA	**CUSTOMS DECLARATION**
CARINARNICA	**CUSTOMS OFFICE**

I only have personal belongings
Imam samo predmete za osebno uporabo
*ee-**mam** sa-mo pred-**me**-te za o-**seb**-no oo-po-**ra**-bo*

Do I have to pay duty on this?
Ali moram za to plačati carino?
*a-lee **mo**-ram za to **pla**-cha-tee tsa-**ree**-no*

I bought this as a gift *(man)* *(woman)*
To sem kupil za darilo
*to sem **koo**-pee^w za da-**ree**-lo*

To sem kupila za darilo
*to sem koo-**pee**-la za da-**ree**-lo*

■ YOU MAY HEAR

Imate kaj za prijaviti?
*ee-**ma**-te ka^y za pree-**ya**-vee-tee*
Have you anything to declare?

Za to boste morali plačati carino
*za to **bos**-te **mo**-ral-ee **pla**-cha-tee tsa-**ree**-no*
We'll have to charge you duty on this

■ AIRPORT ■ ARRIVAL

days

MONDAY	PONEDELJEK
TUESDAY	TOREK
WEDNESDAY	SREDA
THURSDAY	ČETRTEK
FRIDAY	PETEK
SATURDAY	SOBOTA
SUNDAY	NEDELJA

seasons

SPRING	POMLAD
SUMMER	POLETJE
AUTUMN	JESEN
WINTER	ZIMA

months

JANUARY	JANUAR
FEBRUARY	FEBRUAR
MARCH	MAREC
APRIL	APRIL
MAY	MAJ
JUNE	JUNIJ
JULY	JULIJ
AUGUST	AVGUST
SEPTEMBER	SEPTEMBER
OCTOBER	OKTOBER
NOVEMBER	NOVEMBER
DECEMBER	DECEMBER

What is today's date?
Katerega smo danes?
*ka-**tee**-re-ga smo **da**-nes*

Today is 7th April 1997
Danes je sedmi april 1997   (written 7.4.1997)
***da**-nes ye **sed**-mee a-**preel** tee-**soch** de-**vet**-sto **sed**-em-een-dev-**et**-de-set*

on Saturday	**on Saturdays**	**every Saturday**
v soboto	ob sobotah	vsako soboto
*oo so-**bo**-to*	*ob so-**bo**-tah*	*ʷsa-ko so-**bo**-to*

this Saturday	**next Saturday**	**last Saturday**
to soboto	naslednjo soboto	prejšnjo soboto
*to so-**bo**-to*	*nas-**led**-nyo so-**bo**-to*	***preysh**-nyo so-**bo**-to*

in June	**at the beginning of June**
junija	v začetku junija
***yoo**-nee-ya*	*oo za-**chet**-koo **yoo**-nee-ya*

■ NUMBERS

34

DENTIST m/f	ZOBOZDRAVNIK / ZOBOZDRAVNICA
FILLING	PLOMBA
CROWN	KRONA
DENTURES	UMETNO ZOBOVJE / ZOBNA PROTEZA

I need to see a dentist
Moram k zobozdravniku
mo-ram k zo-boz-drav-nee-koo

I have toothache
Imam zobobol
ee-mam zo-bo-bol

This tooth hurts
Ta zob me boli
ta zob me bo-lee

I've lost a filling
Plomba mi je izpadla
plom-ba mee ye eez-pad-la

Can you give me something for the pain?
Mi lahko date nekaj proti bolečinam?
mee la-hko da-te ne-kay pro-tee bo-lech-ee-nam

Do I have to pay?
Ali moram plačati?
a-lee mo-ram pla-cha-tee

How much will it be?
Koliko bo to stalo?
ko-lee-ko bo to sta-lo

Can I have a receipt, please?
Lahko dobim račun, prosim?
la-hko do-beem ra-choon pro-seem

■ **YOU MAY HEAR**

Moral ga bom izpuliti
mo-raʷ ga bom eez-poo-lee-tee
I'll have to take it out

Plombo vam bom napravil
plom-bo vam bom na-pra-veeʷ
I'll have to give you a filling

■ **DOCTOR**

ON THE LEFT	NA LEVO
ON THE RIGHT	NA DESNO
STRAIGHT ON	NARAVNOST
NEXT TO	ZRAVEN
NEAR TO	BLIZU
OPPOSITE	NASPROTI
TRAFFIC LIGHTS	SEMAFOR
CHURCH	CERKEV
SQUARE	TRG
ZEBRA CROSSING	PREHOD ZA PEŠCE
BRIDGE	MOST

Excuse me
Oprostite
o-pro-**stee**-te

How do I get...?
Kako pridem...?
ka-**ko** pree-dem...?

to the station
na železniško postajo
na zhe-**lez**-neesh-ko po-**sta**-yo

to the shops
do trgovin
do trr-go-**veen**

to this museum
v ta muzej
oo ta moo-**zey**

to this village
v to vas
oo to vas

Where is...?
Kje je...?
k^ye ye...

Where are...?
Kje so...?
k^ye so...

Is it far?
Ali je daleč?
a-lee ye **da**-lech

Are we on the right road for...?
Ali smo na pravi cesti za...?
a-lee smo na **pra**-vee **tses**-tee za...

■ **YOU MAY HEAR**

Zavijte na levo
za-**veey**-te na **lev**-o
Turn left

Zavijte na desno
za-**veey**-te na **des**-no
Turn right

Pojdite naravnost po tej cesti
poy-dee-te na-**rav**-nost po tey **tses**-tee
Go straight along this road

■ **BASICS** ■ **MAPS, GUIDES & NEWSPAPERS**

What facilities are there for disabled people?
 Ali obstajajo možnosti za invalide?
 *a-lee ob-**sta**-ya-yo **mozh**-no-stee za een-va-**lee**-de*

Where are the toilets for the disabled?
 Kje so toaletni prostori za invalide?
 *kᵧe so to-a-**let**-nee pro-**sto**-ree za een-va-**lee**-de*

Do you have any bedrooms on the ground floor?
 Imate proste sobe v pritličju?
 *ee-**ma**-te **pro**-ste **so**-be oo preet-**leech**-yoo*

Is there a lift?
 Imate dvigalo?
 *ee-**ma**-te dvee-**ga**-lo*

Where is the lift?
 Kje je dvigalo?
 *kᵧe ye dvee-**ga**-lo*

Are there many stairs?
 Ali je veliko stopnic?
 *a-lee ye ve-**lee**-ko stop-**neets***

How wide is the entrance door?
 Kako široka so vhodna vrata?
 *ka-**ko** shee-**ro**-ka so ᵂ**hod**-na **vra**-ta*

Is the door wide enough for a wheelchair?
 Ali so vrata dovolj široka za invalidski voziček?
 *a-lee so **vra**-ta do-**volʸ** shee-**ro**-ka za een-va-**leed**-skee vo-**zee**-chek*

Is there a reduction for disabled people?
 Ali je za invalide popust?
 *a-lee ye za een-va-**lee**-de po-**poost***

■ **ACCOMMODATION** ■ **HOTEL** ■ **CAMPING**

All tourists have a right to emergency medical aid. If you have to pay for the service you will be given a receipt which should enable you to apply for reimbursement at home.
In larger towns clinics are open from 0700 to 1900. For information about medical services contact **ZDRAVNIŠKA DEŽURNA SLUŽBA** – *the number will be listed at the back of the telephone directory.*

DOCTOR m/f	**ZDRAVNIK / ZDRAVNICA**
HOSPITAL	**BOLNIŠNICA**
CASUALTY DEPT	**URGENTNI ODDELEK**
FIRST AID	**PRVA POMOČ**
AMBULANCE	**REŠILNI AVTO**
DOCTOR ON DUTY...	**DEŽURNI ZDRAVNIK**

I'm not well
Ne počutim se dobro
ne po-**choo**-teem se **do**-bro

I need to see a doctor
Moram k zdravniku
mo-ram k zdrav-**nee**-koo

Where is the nearest clinic?
Kje je najbližja ambulanta?
kʸe ye **naʸ**-bleezh-ya am-boo-**lan**-ta

I have a pain here... *(point)*
Tukaj me boli...
too-kaʸ me bo-**lee**...

My son is ill
Moj sin je bolan
moy seen ye bo-**lan**

My daughter is ill
Moja hčerka je bolna
mo-ya h-**cheer**-ka ye bo**ʷ**-na

I have a temperature
Imam temperaturo
ee-**mam** tem-pe-ra-**too**-ro

He/She has a temperature
Ima temperaturo
ee-**ma** tem-pe-ra-**too**-ro

I'm pregnant
Noseča sem
no-**se**-cha sem

I'm on the Pill
jemljem tablete
yem-lyem tab-**le**-te

I'm diabetic
Sladkorni bolnik sem
slad-**kor**-nee bol-**neek** sem

I have high-blood pressure
imam visok krvni pritisk
ee-**mam** vee-**sok krrv**-nee pree-**tseesk**

I'm allergic to... *(man)*
Alergičen sem na...
a-**ler**-gee-chen sem na...

(woman)
Alergična sem na...
a-**ler**-gee-chna sem na...

Will he have to go to hospital?
Ali bo moral v bolnišnico?
a-lee bo **mo**-ra^w oo bol-**neesh**-nee-tso

When are visiting hours?
Kdaj so obiski?
kda^y so o-**bee**-skee

My... / His... / Her...
Moja... / Njegova... / Njena...
mo-ya... / n^{y}e-**go**-va... / n^{y}e-na...

blood group is...
krvna skupina je...
krrv-na skoo-**pee**-na -ye...

■ **YOU MAY HEAR**

Napisal vam bom recept
na-**pee**-sa^w vam bom re-**tsept**
I'll write you a prescription

Morali boste v bolnišnico
mo-ra-lee **bos**-te oo bol-**neesh**-nee-tso
You will have to go to the hospital

Ni nič resnega
nee neech **res**-ne-ga
It's nothing serious

■ **BODY** ■ **EMERGENCIES** ■ **PHARMACY**

Coffee is drunk at all hours. It is usually strong, black and sweet (espresso style). You might find tea weak and rather tasteless.

a coffee	**a tea**	**a lager**	**...please**
kavo	čaj	pivo	...prosim
ka-vo	*cha**	***pee**-vo*	*...pro-seem*

with milk	**with lemon**	**with ice**
z mlekom	z limono	z ledom
*z **mle**-kom*	*z lee-**mo**-no*	*z-**le**-dom*

with sugar	**without sugar**
s sladkorjem	brez sladkorja
*s-slad-**kor**-yem*	*brez slad-**kor**-ya*

a glass of...	**a bottle of...**
kozarec...	steklenico...
*ko-**za**-rets...*	*ste-kle-**nee**-tso...*

mineral water	**sparkling**	**still**
mineralne vode	gazirane	negazirane
*mee-ne-**ral**-ne **vo**-de*	*ga-**zee**-ra-ne*	*ne-ga-**zee**-ra-ne*

I'm paying!
Jaz plačam!
*yaz **pla**-cham*

■ YOU MAY HEAR

Želite, prosim?	Kaj boste pili?
*zhe-**lee**-te pro-seem*	*ka* **bos**-te **pee**-lee*
Can I help you?	**What will you have to drink?**

■ OTHER DRINKS

wine	vino
hot chocolate	kakav
fruit juice	sadni sok
apple juice	jabolčni sok
orange juice	pomarančni sok

40

Slovenia offers a variety of eating places from simple snack bars to luxury restaurants. Menus often include English, Italian and German translations of dishes.

BIFE *a snack bar, usually found at stations, in shopping centres. They serve hot and cold food.*

BISTRO *a small restaurant, offering reasonably-priced meals.*

GOSTILNA *an inn, where you can have food and drinks, often serving traditional country food.*

RESTAVRACIJA *a restaurant, prices can vary.*

SAMOPOSTREŽNA RESTAVRACIJA *a self-service restaurant, usually reasonably-priced.*

SLAŠČIČARNA *a cake shop, serving sandwiches, cakes, desserts, tea, coffee and soft drinks. They don't serve alcohol.*

Many places have international names such as 'SNACK BAR', 'PICERIJA' where you can have a meal.

■ MEALS

BREAKFAST ZAJTRK *Slovenes do not eat much at breakfast: a small cup of strong coffee and perhaps a piece of toast with butter and jam. In hotels and restaurants you will be able to order a larger meal. Breakfast may be served buffet-style.*

LUNCH KOSILO *This is the main meal of the day and eaten around 1200.*

DINNER VEČERJA *This is usually a lighter meal eaten around 1900-2000.*

CONT...

Can you recommend a good restaurant?
Mi lahko priporočite kakšno dobro restavracijo?
mee la-**hko** pree-po-**ro**-chee-te **kak**-shno **do**-bro re-staw-**ra**-tsee-yo

I'd like to reserve a table... *(man)* *(woman)*
Rad bi rezerviral mizo...
rad bee re-zer-**vee**-raw **mee**-zo...

Rada bi rezervirala mizo...
ra-da bee re-zer-**vee**-ra-la **mee**-zo

at 7 o'clock	at 8 o'clock	Waiter! / Waitress!
ob sedmih	ob osmih	Natakar! / Natakarica!
ob **sed**-mee-h	ob **os**-mee-h	na-**ta**-kar / na-**ta**-ka-ree-tsa

The menu, please
Jedilni list, prosim
ye-**deel**-nee leest pro-seem

Can we sit...?	**by the window**	**on the terrace**
Bi lahko sedeli...?	pri oknu	na terasi
bee la-**hko** se-**de**-lee...	pree **ok**-noo	na te-**ra**-see

Can we have...?	**more water**	**some butter**
Bi lahko dobili...?	še vode	malo masla
bee la-**hko** do-**bee**-lee	she **vo**-de	**ma**-lo **mas**-la

	more bread	**an ashtray**
	še kruha	pepelnik
	she **kroo**-ha	pe-**pel**-neek

	another chair	**another plate**
	še en stol	še en krožnik
	she en sto^w	she en **krozh**-neek

Do you have...?	**anything special for children**
Ali imate...?	kaj posebnega za otroke
a-lee ee-**ma**-te...	ka^y po-**seb**-ne-ga za o-**tro**-ke

	some typical Slovene dishes
	kakšne pristne slovenske jedi
	kak-shne **preest**-ne slo-**ven**-ske ye-**dee**

What do you recommend?
  Kaj priporočate?
  kaY pree-po-ro-cha-te

What is this?
  Kaj je to?
  kaY ye to

I'd like something light
  Rad(a) bi nekaj malega
  rad(a) bee ne-kaY ma-le-ga

I'm on a diet
  Imam dieto
  ee-mam dee-ye-to

What is the speciality of the house?
  Kaj je hišna specialiteta?
  kaY ye heesh-na spe-tsee-a-lee-te-ta

Can I order, please
  Lahko naročim, prosim
  la-hko na-ro-cheem pro-seem

Can I smoke here?
  Lahko tukaj kadim?
  la-hko too-kaY ka-deem

Where is the non-smoking area?
  Kje so nekadilci?
  kYe so ne-ka-deel-tsee

The bill, please
  Račun, prosim
  ra-choon pro-seem

We're paying separately
  Plača vsak zase
  pla-cha Wsak za-se

■YOU MAY HEAR

Kaj želite naročiti?
kaY zhe-lee-te na-ro-chee-tee
What would you like to order?

Priporočam vam...
pree-po-ro-cham vam...
I recommend...

Kaj boste pili?
kaY bos-te pee-lee
What would you like to drink?

Nimamo...
nee-ma-mo...
We don't have...

Ali bi...
a-lee bee...
Would you like...

CONT...

■ **JEDILNI LIST**   **MENU**

HLADNE PREDJEDI	**COLD STARTERS**
TOPLE PREDJEDI	**HOT STARTERS**

■ **JUHE**   **SOUPS** soup is a common starter in Slovenia, especially in the winter.

ČISTA JUHA	**clear soup** (bouillon)
GOBOVA JUHA	**mushroom soup**
GOVEJA JUHA Z REZANCI	**beef soup with noodles**
FIŽOLOVA JUHA	**bean soup**
KOKOŠJA JUHA	**chicken soup**
KROMPIRJEVA JUHA	**potato soup**
PARADIŽNIKOVA JUHA	**tomato soup**
ZELENJAVNA JUHA	**vegetable soup**

Most places will have the option between dishes to order and ready-cooked dishes. The difference is that the dishes to order are usually more elaborate and you may have to wait for them a bit longer. Below are some examples of both.

■ **JEDI PO NAROČILU**   **DISHES TO ORDER**

MEŠANO MESO V OMAKI	**mixed meat in gravy**
NADEVAN PIŠČANEC	**stuffed chicken**
TELEČJA PEČENKA	**roast veal**

■ **GOTOVE JEDI**   **READY-COOKED DISHES**

NADEVANA PAPRIKA	**stuffed peppers**
KISLO ZELJE IN KLOBASE	**sauerkraut and sausages**
DUNAJSKI ZREZEK	**veal escalope**

■ **JEDI NA ŽARU**   **GRILLED DISHES**

ZREZEK NA ŽARU	**grilled steak**
MEŠANO MESO NA ŽARU	**grilled mixed meat**
RAŽNJIČI	**sish kebab**
ČEVAPČIČI	**ground meat rolls**

■ TYPES OF MEAT AND POULTRY

DIVJAČINA	game
FAZAN	pheasant
GOVEDINA	beef
GOVEJI GOLAŽ	beef goulash
GOVEJA OBARA	beef stew
GOVEJA PEČENKA	roast beef
JAGNJETINA	lamb
JETRA	liver
JEZIK	tongue
KURJA OBARA	chicken stew
MESO	meat
NADEVAN PURAN	stuffed turkey
NADEVAN PIŠČANEC	stuffed chicken
PEČENA KURA/PIŠČANEC	roast chicken
PERUTNINA	poultry
POHANA KURA/PIŠČANEC	fried chicken in breadcrumbs
PIŠČANEC	chicken
PRŠUT	cured ham
PURAN	turkey
RACA	duck
SVINJINA	pork
SVINJSKA PEČENKA	roast pork
SVINJSKI KOTLET	pork chop
TELEČJA PEČENKA	roast veal
TELETINA	veal
ZAJEC	rabbit

■ JAJCA EGGS

OCVRTA JAJCA	fried eggs
OCVRTA JAJCA S ŠUNKO	fried eggs with ham
OCVRTA JAJCA S SLANINO	fried eggs with bacon
OMLETA S SIROM	cheese omelette
OMLETA S ŠUNKO	ham omelette

CONT...

■ RIBE/MORSKI SADEŽI — FISH AND SEAFOOD

JASTOG	**lobster**
JEGULJA	**eel**
KALAMARI	**squid**
KRAP	**carp**
LIGNJI	**squid**
LOSOS	**salmon**
RAKI	**lobster**
RIBE	**fish**
SARDINE	**sardines**
ŠKOLJKE	**shellfish**
SVEŽE POSTRVI	**fresh trout**

■ PRILOGE/ZELENJAVA — SIDE DISHES/VEGETABLES

BELUŠ	**asparagus**
CMOKI	**dumplings**
CVETAČA	**cauliflower**
GRAH	**peas**
FIŽOL	**beans**
KORENJE	**carrots**
KROMPIR	**potatoes**
KRUHOVI CMOKI	**bread dumplings**
MAKARONI	**macaroni**
MARELIČNI CMOKI	**apricot dumplings**
MEŠANA ZELENJAVA	**mixed vegetables**
PEČEN KROMPIR V PEČICI	**baked potatoes**
PIRE KROMPIR	**mashed potatoes**
POMMES FRITES	**French fries**
MASLEN KROMPIR	**sauté potatoes**
RDEČA PESA	**beets**
REPA	**turnip**

PRAŽEN KROMPIR	fried potatoes with onions
RIŽ	rice
RIŽ Z GOBAMI	rice with mushrooms
RIŽ Z GRAHOM	rice with peas
SIROVI CMOKI	cheese dumplings
ŠPINAČA	spinach
ŠPAGETI	spaghetti
TESTENINE	pasta
ZELJE	cabbage
ZÉLENA	celery

■ SOLATE — **SALADS**

FIŽOLOVA SOLATA	bean salad
KROMPIRJEVA SOLATA	potato salad
KUMARE V SOLATI	cucumber salad
MEŠANA SOLATA	mixed salad
RUSKA SOLATA	Russian salad
SEZONSKA SOLATA	salad made of vegetables in season
ZELENA SOLATA	green salad
ZELJNATA SOLATA	coleslaw

■ SLAŠČICE — **DESSERT**

PALAČINKE	pancakes
POTICA	roulade filled with walnuts and raisins traditionally eaten at Christmas and at other festivities
PREKMURSKA GIBANICA	strudel filled with nuts, apples, cream cheese and poppy seeds
SLADOLED	ice cream
SADNA KUPA	fruit salad
ŠTRUKLJI	roulade *(can be sweet or savoury)*
TORTE	gateaux

■ DRINKING ■ VEGETARIAN ■ WINES & SPIRITS

POLICE	POLICIJA	*tel: 92*
FIRE BRIGADE	GASILCI	*tel: 93*
FIRST AID	PRVA POMOČ	*tel: 94*
AMZ	*(equivalent to AA)*	*tel: 987*

Help!
Na pomoč!
*na po-**moch***

Fire!
Požar!
*po-**zhar***

Can you help me?
Mi lahko pomagate?
*mee la-**hko** po-**ma**-ga-te*

There has been an accident!
Pripetila se je nesreča!
*pree-pe-**tee**-la se ye nes-**re**-cha*

Someone has been injured
Nekdo se je ponesrečil
*nek-**do** se ye po-nes-**re**-chee^w*

Please call...
Prosim pokličite...
*pro-seem po-**klee**-chee-te...*

the police
policijo
*po-lee-**tsee**-yo*

a doctor
zdravnika
*zdrav-**nee**-ka*

an ambulance
rešilni avto
*re-**sheel**-nee a^w-to*

Someone has stolen my...
Nekdo mi je ukradel...
*nek-**do** mee ye oo-**kra**-de^w*

passport
potni list
***pot**-nee leest*

handbag
torbico
***tor**-bee-tso*

money
denar
*de-**nar***

wallet
denarnico
*de-**nar**-nee-tso*

travellers cheques
potovalne čeke
*po-to-**val**-ne **che**-ke*

My car has been broken into
Vlomili so mi v avto
*vlo-**mee**-lee so me oo a^w-to*

My car has been stolen
Ukradli so mi avto
oo-**krad**-lee so mee **aw**-to

I've been raped
Posilili so me
po-**see**-lee-lee so me

Where is the police station?
Kje je policijska postaja?
kᵞe ye po-lee-**tseey**-ska po-**sta**-ya

I want to report a crime (man)
Rad bi prijavil zločin
rad bee pree-**ya**-veew zlo-**cheen**

(woman)
Rada bi prijavila zločin
ra-da bee pree-**ya**-vee-la zlo-**cheen**

I want to speak to a police woman / woman doctor
Rada bi govorila s policistko / z zdravnico
ra-da bee go-vo-**ree**-la s-po-lee-**tseest**-ko /z-zdrav-**nee**-tso

I need to make a phone call
Telefonirati moram
te-le-fo-**nee**-ra-tee **mo**-ram

How much is the fine?
Koliko je kazen?
ko-lee-ko ye **ka**-zen

Where do I have to pay it?
Kje moram plačati?
k-ye **mo**-ram **pla**-cha-tee

Do I have to pay it straightaway?
Ali moram plačati takoj?
a-lee **mo**-ram **pla**-cha-tee ta-**koy**

I'm very sorry!
Zelo mi je žal!
ze-**lo** mee ye zha**w**

■ BODY ■ DOCTOR

49

There are many cultural events throughout the year. Contact the tourist information office for their excellent literature.

Do you have a programme of events?
Imate program prireditev?
ee-**ma**-te pro-**gram** pree-re-**dee**-teʷ

What is there to do in the evenings?
Kaj se dogaja ob večerih?
kaʸ se do-**ga**-ya ob ve-**che**-ree-h

Is there anything for children?
Je kaj primernega za otroke?
ye kaʸ pree-**meer**-ne-ga za o-**tro**-ke

Where can I get tickets for tonight?
Kje lahko kupim vstopnice za danes zvečer?
kʸe la-**hko koo**-peem ʷstop-nee-tse za **da**-nes zve-**cheer**

I'd like ... tickets	**... for adults**	**... for children**
Rad(a) bi ... vstopnice	... za odrasle	... za otroke
rad(a) bee ... ʷstop-nee-tse	... za o-**dras**-le	... za o-**tro**-ke

Where is a night club?
Kje je kakšen nočni bar?
kʸe ye **kak**-shen **noch**-nee bar

How much does it cost to get in?
Koliko je vstopnina?
ko-lee-ko je ʷstop-**nee**-na

Are there any free shows in town?
Je v mestu kakšna predstava, kjer je vstop prost?
ye oo **mes**-too **kak**-shna pred-**sta**-va, kyeer ye oos-**top** prost

What is on at the weekend?
Kaj se dogaja čez konec tedna?
kaʸ se do-**ga**-ya chez **ko**-nets **ted**-na

■ CINEMA ■ SIGHTSEEING & TOURIST OFFICE ■ THEATRE

ADDRESSING A FAX

FAX NUMBER:	ŠT. FAXA:
TO:	PREJME:
FROM:	POŠILJA:
RE:	ZADEVA:
PAGE...OF...	STRAN...OD SKUPAJ...
PLEASE FIND ATTACHED...	PRILOŽENO...
MESSAGE:	SPOROČILO:

Do you have a fax?
Imate fax?
*ee-**ma**-te faks*

I want to send a fax *(man)*
Rad bi poslal fax
*rad bee po-**sla**[w] faks*

(woman)
Rada bi poslala fax
***ra**-da bee po-**sla**-la faks*

What is your fax number?
Kakšna je številka vašega faxa?
***kak**-shna ye shte-**veel**-ka **va**-sheg-a **fak**-sa*

I'm having trouble getting through to your fax
Ne dobim zveze z vašim faxom
*ne do-**beem** **zve**-ze z **va**-sheem **fak**-som*

Please resend your fax
Prosim, pošljite ga še enkrat
*pro-seem **posh**-lyee-te ga she **en**-krat*

I can't read it
Ne vidi se
*ne **vee**-dee se*

Your fax is constantly engaged
Vaš fax je neprestano zaseden
*vash faks ye ne-pre-**sta**-no za-**se**-den*

■ LETTERS ■ TELEPHONE

biscuits	piškoti	peesh-**ko**-tee
bread (white)	beli kruh	**be**-lee kroo-h
bread (brown)	črni kruh	**chrr**-nee kroo-h
bread roll	žemlja	**zhem**-lya
butter	maslo	**mas**-lo
cheese	sir	seer
chicken	piščanec / kura	peesh-**cha**-nets / **koo**-ra
coffee	kava	**ka**-va
cream	smetana	**sme**-ta-na
crisps	čips	cheeps
eggs	jajca	ya**y**-tsa
fish	ribe	**ree**-be
flour	moka	**mo**-ka
ham	šunka	**shoon**-ka
honey	med	med
jam	marmelada	mar-me-**la**-da
juice	sok	sok
margarine	margarina	mar-ga-**ree**-na
marmalade	pomarančna marmelada	po-ma-**ranch**-na mar-me-**la**-da
meat	meso	me-**so**
milk	mleko	**mle**-ko
mustard	gorčica	gor-**chee**-tsa
oil	olje	**ol**-ye
pepper	poper	**po**-per
rice	riž	reezh
salt	sol	so**w**
sugar	sladkor	**slad**-kor
stock cubes	jušne kocke	**yoosh**-ne **kots**-ke
tea	čaj	cha**y**
a tin of...	konzerva...	kon-**ser**-va...
vinegar	kis	kees
yoghurt	jogurt	**yo**-goort

Fruit
Sadje
sa-d^ye

Where can I buy fruit?
Kje lahko kupim sadje?
k^ye la-**hko koo**-peem **sa**-d^ye

4 apples, please
Štiri jabolka, prosim
shtee-ree ya-**bo^w**-ka pro-seem

Half a kilo of cherries
Pol kilograma češenj
po^w kee-lo-**gra**-ma **che**-shen^y

apples	jabolka	ya-**bo^w**-ka
apricots	marelice	ma-**re**-lee-tse
bananas	banane	ba-**na**-ne
blackcurrants	črni ribez	**chrr**-nee **ree**-bez
cherries	češnje	**chesh**-n^ye
grapefruit	grenivka	gre-**nee^w**-ka
grapes	grozdje	**groz**-d^ye
kiwi fruit	kivi	**kee**-vee
lemon	limona	lee-**mo**-na
melon	melona	me-**lo**-na
nectarines	medovnate breskve	me-**do^w**-na-te **bre**-skve
oranges	pomaranče	po-ma-**ran**-che
peaches	breskve	**bresk**-ve
pears	hruške	**hroosh**-ke
plums	slive	**slee**-ve
raspberries	maline	ma-**lee**-ne
strawberries	jagode	**ya**-go-de
tangerines	mandarine	man-da-**ree**-ne
watermelon	lubenica	loo-be-**nee**-tsa

■ **FOOD–VEGETABLES** ■ **PAYING** ■ **SHOPS**

Vegetables
  Zelenjava
  ze-len-**ya**-va

Where can I buy vegetables?
  Kye lahko kupim zelenjavo?
  k^ye la-**hko koo**-peem ze-len-**ya**-vo

Half a kilo of carrots
  Pol kilograma korenja
  po^W kee-lo-**gra**-ma ko-**ren**-ya

Quarter of a kilo of mushrooms
  Četrt kilograma gob
  che-**trrt** kee-lo-**gra**-ma gob

asparagus	beluš	be-**loosh**
aubergine	melancana	me-lan-**tsa**-na
beans	fižol	fee-**zho**^w
beets	rdeča pesa	rr-**de**-cha **pe**-sa
cabbage	zelje	**zel**-ye
carrots	korenje	ko-**ren**-ye
cauliflower	cvetača	tsve-**ta**-cha
celery	zélena	**ze**-le-na
courgettes	bučke	**booch**-ke
cucumber	kumara	**koo**-ma-ra
garlic	česen	**che**-sen
leeks	por	por
mushrooms	gobe	**go**-be
onions	čebula	che-**boo**-la
peas	grah	gra-h
pepper (green)	paprika	**pa**-pree-ka
potatoes	krompir	krom-**peer**
salad	solata	so-**la**-ta
spinach	špinača	shpee-**na**-cha
tomatoes	paradižnik	pa-ra-**deezh**-neek
turnips	repa	**re**-pa

■ **FOOD—GENERAL/FRUIT** ■ **PAYING** ■ **SHOPS**

Good day (hello)
 Dober dan
 do-ber dan

Goodbye
 Na svidenje
 na **svee**-den-ye

Bye
 Adijo
 a-**dee**-yo

Good morning
 Dobro jutro
 do-bro **yoo**-tro

Good afternoon / evening (after about 5pm)
 Dober večer
 do-ber ve-**cheer**

Good night
 Lahko noč
 la-**hko** noch

How are you?
 Kako vam gre?
 ka-**ko** vam gre

Fine, thanks, and you?
 Dobro, hvala, in vam?
 do-bro **hva**-la een vam

Fine, thanks
 Dobro, hvala
 do-bro **hva**-la

Let me introduce you to Mr... / Mrs...
 Naj vam predstavim gospoda… / gospo…
 naᵞ vam pred-**sta**-veem gos-**po**-da… / gos-**po**…

Pleased to meet you
 Me veseli
 me ve-se-**lee**

How do you do
 Pozdravljeni
 poz-**dra**ʷ-lᵞe-nee

See you tomorrow
 Vidimo se jutri
 vee-dee-mo se **yoo**-tree

■ BASICS ■ MAKING FRIENDS

These phrases are intended for use at the hotel desk. More details about rooms can be found in the ACCOMMODATION topic.

CHECK -IN	PRIJAVA	LIFT	DVIGALO
RECEPTION	RECEPCIJA	BREAKFAST ROOM	ZAJTRKOVALNICA
RECEPTIONIST	RECEPTOR(KA)	DINING ROOM	JEDILNICA

I booked a room *(man)*
  Rezerviral sem sobo
  *re-zer-**vee**-ra^w sem **so**-bo*

        (woman)
  Rezervirala sem sobo
  *re-zer-**vee**-ra-la sem **so**-bo*

My name is...
  Ime mi je...
  *ee-**me** mee ye...*

The key, please
  Ključ, prosim
  klyooch pro-seem

Room number...
  Številka sobe...
  *shte-**veel**-ka **so**-be...*

Please put this in the safe for me
  Prosim, shranite to v trezorju
  *pro-seem **shra**-nee-te to oo tre-**zor**-yoo*

Please wake me at...
  Zbudite me, prosim, ob...
  *zboo-**dee**-te me pro-seem ob...*

When is...?
  Kdaj je...?
  kda^y ye...

breakfast
  zajtrk
  za^y-trrk

dinner
  večerja
  *ve-**cheer**-ya*

Please prepare the bill
  Prosim pripravite mi račun
  *pro-seem pree-**pra**-vee-te mee ra-**choon***

I'm leaving tomorrow
  Odpotujem jutri
  *od-po-**too**-yem **yoo**-tree*

■ **YOU MAY HEAR**

Bi mi prosim povedali svoje ime?
*bee mee pro-seem po-**ve**-da-lee **svo**-ye ee-**me***
May I have your name?

Številka vaše sobe je...
*shte-**veel**-ka **va**-she **so**-be ye...*
Your room number is...

■ **ACCOMMODATION** ■ **ROOM SERVICE**

Slovenia offers wonderful opportunities for short and long distance walks. Routes are well-marked and you can stay overnight in mountain lodges with dormitory-style accommodation. Contact the Alpine Association of Slovenia for further details: 6100 Ljubljana, Dvorzakova 9, Slovenia, tel: 061 312 553, fax: 061 132 2140. Tourist offices will also have maps.

Could you recommend a route to...
Bi mi lahko priporočili pot do…
bee mee la-**hko** pree-po-**ro**-chee-lee pot do…

Do we need...?
Ali potrebujemo…?
a-lee po-tre-**boo**-ye-mo…

waterproofs
nepremočljiva oblačila
ne-pre-moch-**lyee**-va o-bla-**chee**-la

walking boots
planinske čevlje
pla-**neens**-ke **chev**-lʸe

a sleeping bag
spalno vrečo
spal-no **vre**-cho

Where can we stay overnight?
Kje bi lahko prenočili?
kʸe bee la-**hko** pre-no-**chee**-lee

How far is it to...?
Kako daleč je do…?
ka-ko **da**-lech ye do…

Approximately how long will it take me?
Približno kako dolgo bom hodil(a)?
pree-**bleezh**-no ka-**ko** do^w-go bom **ho**-dee^w(-dee-la)

Is it steep?
Je strmo?
ye **strr**-mo

What time does it get dark?
Ob kateri uri se stemni?
ob ka-**tee**-ree **oo**-ree se stem-**nee**

Is there an inn on the way?
Je na poti kakšna gostilna?
ye na **po**-tee **kak**-shna go-**steel**-na

■DIRECTIONS ■MAPS, GUIDES & NEWSPAPERS

Whereas in English 'dear' is used for addressing everybody, Slovenes make a distinction according to the closeness of the relationship. You use 'dear' for friends and close acquaintances, and Spoštovana (for women), Spoštovani (for men) when you don't know the person very well or not at all.
Also note that in Slovene the exclamation mark is used where in English you would use a comma. Pronouns (e.g. you, your) are usually capitalized to indicate respect.

27th March 1998	27.3.1998
Dear Sirs	Spoštovani!
Dear Mr....,	Spoštovani gospod...!
Dear Mrs...,	Spoštovana gospa...!
Dear Marko,	Dragi Marko!
Dear Maria,	Draga Marija!
Yours faithfully	S spoštovanjem
Yours sincerely	S spoštovanjem
Best regards	Lep pozdrav
Love	S prisrčnimi pozdravi

Please find enclosed... V prilogi pošiljamo...

Thank you for your letter of 7 May Hvala za Vaš dopis od 7. maja

I look forward to hearing from you V pričakovanju Vašega odgovora

■ FAX ■ OFFICE

BAGGAGE RECLAIM	PRRTLJAGA
LEFT-LUGGAGE	GARDEROBA
TROLLEY	VOZIČEK

My luggage hasn't arrived
Moja prtljaga ni prispela
mo-ya prrt-*lya*-ga nee prees-*pe*-la

What has happened to the luggage on the flight from...?
Kaj se je zgodilo s prtljago poleta iz...?
ka^y se ye zgo-*dee*-lo s-prrt-*lya*-go po-*le*-ta eez...

Would you please help me carry...
Bi mi prosim pomagali nesti...
bee mee pro-*seem* po-*ma*-ga-lee *nes*-tee...

my luggage	**this bag**	**this suitcase**
mojo prtljago	to torbo	ta kovček
mo-yo prrt-*lya*-go	to *tor*-bo	ta *ko^w*-chek

How much do I owe you?
Koliko vam dolgujem?
ko-lee-ko vam do^w-*goo*-yem

Where are the luggage trolleys?
Kje so vozički za prtljago?
k^ye so vo-*zeech*-kee za prrt-*lya*-go

Can we leave our luggage here?
Ali lahko pustimo tukaj našo prtljago?
a-lee la-*hko* poos-*tee*-mo *too*-ka^y na-sho prrt-*lya*-go

We'd like to leave it here...
Tukaj bi jo radi pustili...
too-ka^y bee yo *ra*-dee poo-*stee*-lee...

overnight	**for...hours**
čez noč	za...ur
chez noch	za...oor

What's your name?
Kako vam je ime? *(polite)*
ka-ko vam ye ee-**me**

Kako ti je ime? *(familiar)*
ka-ko tee ye ee-**me**

My name is...
Ime mi je...
ee-**me** mee ye...

I'd like to introduce...
Vam lahko predstavim...
vam la-**hko** pred-**sta**-veem...

This is...
To je...
to ye...

How old are you?
Koliko si star? *(familiar)*
ko-lee-ko see star

I am ... years old
Star sem ... let
star sem ... let

Where are you from?
Od kod prihajate? *(polite)*
od kod pree-**ha**-ya-te

I'm from...
Sem iz...
sem eez...

England	Scotland	Wales	Ireland
Anglije	Škotske	Walesa	Irske
an-glee-ye	**shkot**-ske	**wel**-sa	**eer**-ske

Where do you live?
Kje živite? *(polite)*
k^ye zhee-**vee**-te

I live in...
Živim v...
zhee-**veem** oo...

I'm at school
Hodim v šolo
ho-deem oo sho-lo

I work
Delam
de-lam

I'm retired *(man)*
Upokojen sem
oo-po-ko-**yen** sem

(woman)
Upokojena sem
oo-po-ko-**ye**-na sem

I'm ...	**married**	**divorced**
Sem...	poročen (poročena)	ločen (ločena)
sem...	po-ro-**chen** (po-ro-**che**-na)	**lo**-chen (**lo**-che-na)
	I'm widowed *(man)*	*(woman)*
	Vdovec sem	Vdova sem
	vdo-vets sem	**vdo**-va sem

I have...
Imam...
*ee-**mam**...*

a boyfriend
fanta
***fan**-ta*

a girlfriend
punco
***poon**-tso*

a partner *(male)*
soproga
*so-**pro**-ga*

a partner *(female)*
soprogo
*so-**pro**-go*

I have ... children
Imam ... otrok
*ee-**mam** ... o-**trok***

I don't have children
Nimam otrok
nee**-mam o-**trok

I'm here...
Tukaj sem...
***too**-ka^y sem...*

on holiday
na dopustu
*na do-**poos**-too*

on business
službeno
***sloozh**-be-no*

for the weekend
čez konec tedna
*chez **ko**-nets **ted**-na*

Is this your first visit here?
Ste prvič tukaj? *(polite)*
*ste **prr**-veech **too**-ka^y*

Do you like it here?
Vam je všeč? *(polite)*
vam ye ^wshech

Yes, I like it very much
Ja, zelo mi je všeč
*ya ze-**lo** mee ye ^wshech*

No, I don't like it
Ne, ni mi všeč
ne nee mee ^wshech

What do you do in your spare time?
Kaj delate v prostem času? *(polite)*
*ka^y **de**-la-te oo **pros**-tem **cha**-soo*

Do you travel a lot?
Ali veliko potujete? *(polite)*
*a-lee ve-**lee**-ko po-**too**-ye-te*

■ BASICS ■ GREETINGS

Local tourist offices usually have a good stock of maps.

ROAD MAP	CESTNA KARTA
NEWSPAPER	ČASOPIS
MAGAZINE	REVIJA

Do you have a map of the town?
Imate zemljevid mesta?
*ee-**ma**-te zem-l^ye-**veed mes**-ta*

Do you have a map of the region?
Imate zemljevid regije?
*ee-**ma**-te zem-l^ye-**veed re**-gee-ye*

Could you point on the map, where ... is?
Bi mi pokazali na zemljevidu, kje je ...?
*bee mee po-**ka**-za-lee na ze-ml^ye-**vee**-doo k^ye ye...*

Do you have leaflets in English?
Imate brošure v angleščini?
*ee-**ma**-te bro-**shoo**-re oo an-**glesh**-chee-nee*

I'd like this in English
To bi rad(a) v angleščini
*to bee rad(a) oo an-**glesh**-chee-nee*

Do you sell English newspapers?
Ali prodajate angleške časopise?
*a-lee pro-**da**-ya-te an-**glesh**-ke cha-so-**pee**-se*

Do you have any English magazines?
Imate angleške revije?
*ee-**ma**-te an-**glesh**-ke re-**vee**-ye*

Do you have any English books?
Imate angleške knjige?
*ee-**ma**-te an-**glesh**-ke **knee**-ge*

■ DIRECTIONS ■ SIGHTSEEING & TOURIST OFFICE

1 lb = approx. 0.5 kilo   1 pint = approx. 0.5 litre

■ LIQUIDS

1/2 litre of...	pol litra...	po^w lee-tra...
a litre of...	en liter...	en **lee**-ter...
1/2 bottle of...	pol steklenice...	po^w stek-le-**nee**-tse...
a bottle of...	steklenico...	stek-le-**nee**-tso...
a glass of...	kozarec...	ko-**za**-rets...

■ WEIGHTS

100 grams...	sto gramov...	sto **gra**-mo^w...
1/2 kilo of...	pol kilograma...	po^w kee-lo-**gra**-ma...
a kilo of...	en kilogram...	en kee-lo-**gram**...
2 kilos of...	dva kilograma...	dva kee-lo-**gra**-ma...

■ FOOD

a slice of...	en kos...	en kos...
a portion of...	eno porcijo...	**e**-no **por**-tsee-yo...
a box of...	eno škatlo...	**e**-no **shkat**-lo...
a tin of...	eno konzervo...	**e**-no kon-**zer**-vo...

■ MISCELLANEOUS

a half	polovica	po-lo-**vee**-tsa
a third	tretjina	tret-**yee**-na
a quarter	četrtina	che-trr-**tee**-na
more than	več kot	vech kot
less than	manj kot	man^y kot
once	enkrat	en-krat
twice	dva krat	dva krat
three times	tri krat	tree krat

■ **FOOD** ■ **SHOPPING**

*Banks are open Mon. to Fri., 0830-1230, 1400-1630 and on Saturdays from 0830-1200. You can also change money in hotels, at petrol stations, tourist offices and many smaller independent exchange offices. You can often pay in foreign currency as many cash tills are computerized and convert the amount to the currency you wish to pay in. However you will receive change in Slovenian currency **tolars** (1 tolar = 100 stotins).*

BANK	**BANKA**
BUREAU DE CHANGE	**MENJALNICA**
TRAVELLER'S CHEQUES	**POTOVALNI ČEKI**
CREDIT CARD	**KREDITNA KARTICA**
CASH POINT	**BANČNI AVTOMAT**

Where is...?   **the bank**   **the bureau de change**
Kje je ...?   banka   menjalnica
kYe ye...   ***ban**-ka*   *men-**yal**-nee-tsa*

Can I change money here?
Lahko tukaj menjam denar?
*la-**hko** too-kaY **men**-yam de-**nar***

I want to change these traveller's cheques *(man)*
Rad bi zamenjal potovalne čeke
*rad bee za-**men**-yaᵂ po-to-**val**-ne **che**-ke*

I want to change these traveller's cheques *(woman)*
Rada bi zamenjala potovalne čeke
*ra-da bee za-**men**-ya-la po-to-**val**-ne **che**-ke*

Can I pay with...?   **traveller's cheques**
Lahko plačam s...?   potovalnimi čeki
*la-**hko** **pla**-cham s...*   *po-to-**val**-nee-mee **che**-kee*

                                   this credit card
                                     to kreditno kartico
                                     *to kre-**deet**-no **kar**-tee-tso*

■ **PAYING**

Slovenia has a great many musical events and festivals. Contact the tourist information office for details.

Where is the concert hall?
Kje je koncertna dvorana?
*k^ye ye kon-**tsert**-na dvo-**ra**-na*

Where is the opera house?
Kje je opera?
*k^ye ye **o**-pe-ra*

Is there a good concert on in town?
Je v mestu kakšen dober koncert?
*ye oo **mes**-too **kak**-shen **do**-ber kon-**tsert***

Where can I get tickets?
Kje lahko kupimo vstopnice?
*k^ye la-**hko koo**-pee-mo ^w**stop**-nee-tse*

What sort of music do you like?
Kakšna glasba vam je všeč?
***kak**-shna **glas**-ba vam ye ^wshech*

I like...	classical music	jazz	rock
Všeč mi je...	**klasična glasba**	**jazz**	**rok**
^wshech mee ye...	***kla**-seech-na **gla**-sba*	*jazz*	*rock*

Do you like...?
Vam je všeč...?
vam ye ^wshech...

Do you play a musical instrument?
Igrate kakšen instrument?
*ee-**gra**-te kak-shen **een**-stroo-**ment***

I play...	the piano	the guitar
Igram...	**klavir**	**kitaro**
*ee-**gram**...*	*kla-**veer***	*kee-**ta**-ro*

■ ENTERTAINMENT ■ SIGHTSEEING & TOURIST OFFICE

0	nula	**noo**-la
1	ena	**e**-na
2	dva	d**va**
3	tri	tree
4	štiri	**shtee**-ree
5	pet	pet
6	šest	shest
7	sedem	**se**-dem
8	osem	**o**-sem
9	devet	de-**vet**
10	deset	de-**set**
11	enajst	e-**na^y^st**
12	dvanajst	dva-**na^y^st**
13	trinajst	tree-**na^y^st**
14	štirinajst	shtee-ree-**na^y^st**
15	petnajst	pet-**na^y^st**
16	šestnajst	shest-**na^y^st**
17	sedemnajst	se-dem-**na^y^st**
18	osemnajst	o-sem-**na^y^st**
19	devetnajst	de-vet-**na^y^st**
20	dvajset	d**va^y^**-set
21	enaindvajset	e-na-een-**dva^y^**-set
22	dvaindvajset	dva-een-**dva^y^**-set
23	triindvajset	tree-een-**dva^y^**-set
24	štiriindvajset	shtee-ree-een-**dva^y^**-set
25	petindvajset	pet-een-**dva^y^**-set
26	šestindvajset	shest-een-**dva^y^**-set
27	sedemindvajset	sedem-een-**dva^y^**-set
28	osemindvajset	o-sem-een-**dva^y^**-set
29	devetindvajset	de-vet-een-**dva^y^**-set
30	trideset	**tree**-de-set

40	štirideset	**shtee**-ree-de-set
50	petdeset	**pet**-de-set
60	šestdeset	**shest**-de-set
70	sedemdeset	se-**dem**-de-set
80	osemdeset	**o-sem**-de-set
90	devetdeset	**de-vet**-de-set
100	sto	sto
110	sto deset	sto de-**set**
1000	tisoč	**tee**-soch
2000	dva tisoč	dva **tee**-soch
million	milijon	mee-lee-**yon**
billion	milijarda	mee-lee-**yar**-da

first	prvi	**prr**-vee
second	drugi	**droo**-gee
third	tretji	**tret**-yee
fourth	četrti	che-**trr**-tee
fifth	peti	**pe**-tee
sixth	šesti	**shes**-tee
seventh	sedmi	**sed**-mee
eighth	osmi	**os**-mee
ninth	deveti	de-**ve**-tee
tenth	deseti	de-**se**-tee

On the first floor
V prvem nadstropju
oo **prr**-vem nad-**strop**-yoo

The first road on the right
Prva ulica na desno
prr-va **oo**-lee-tsa na **des**-no

The first road on the left
Prva ulica na levo
prr-va **oo**-lee-tsa na **le**-vo

SWITCHBOARD	CENTRALA
OFFICE	PISARNA
DIRECTOR m/f	DIREKTOR / DIREKTORICA
SECRETARY	TAJNICA

I'd like to speak to... *(man)*   *(woman)*
Rad bi govoril z...   Rada bi govorila z...
*rad bee go-vo-**ree**w z...*   ***ra**-da bee go-vo-**ree**-la z...*

What time do you start work?
Ob kateri uri začnete delati?
*ob ka-**tee**-ree **oo**-ree zach-**ne**-te **de**-la-tee*

Where is your office?
Kje je vaša pisarna?
*kye ye **va**-sha pee-**sar**-na*

Would you give me the address, please?
Bi mi dali naslov, prosim?
*bee mee **da**-lee na-**slo**w pro-seem*

Could someone type this for me?
Bi mi lahko nekdo to natipkal?
*bee mee la-**hko** nek-**do** to na-**teep**-ka*w

Can you photocopy this for me, please?
Bi mi lahko to prosim fotokopirali, prosim?
*bee mee la-**hko** to pro-seem fo-to-**ko**-pee-ra-lee pro-seem*

■ YOU MAY HEAR

Prosim, sedite
*pro-seem **se**-dee-te*
Please take a seat

Počakajte trenutek, prosim
*po-**cha**-kay-te tre-**noo**-tek pro-seem*
Please wait a moment

■ BUSINESS ■ FAX ■ LETTERS

68

How much is it?
Koliko stane?
***ko**-lee-ko **sta**-ne*

How much are they?
Koliko stanejo?
***ko**-lee-ko **sta**-ne-yo*

I'd like to pay (man)
Rad bi plačal
*rad bee **pla**-cha^w*

(woman)
Rada bi plačala
***ra**-da bee **pla**-cha-la*

Can I pay…?
Lahko plačam…?
*la-**hko pla**-cham…*

by credit card
s kreditno kartico
*s kre-**deet**-no **kar**-tee-tso*

by cheque
s čekom
*s **che**-kom*

Is service included?
Je postrežba vključena?
*ye pos-**trezh**-ba **vklyoo**-che-na*

Can I have a receipt, please
Lahko dobim račun, prosim
*la-**hko** do-**beem** ra-**choon** pro-seem*

I think there is a mistake on this bill
Mislim, da je na tem računu napaka
***mee**-sleem da ye na tem ra-**choo**-noo na-**pa**-ka*

Do I have to pay in advance?
Moram plačati v naprej?
***mo**-ram **pla**-cha-tee oo **nap**-rey*

Sorry, I have no change
Žal mi je, nimam drobiža
*zha^w mee ye **nee**-mam dro-**bee**-zha*

Keep the change
Obdržite drobiž
*ob-**drr**-zhee-te dro-**beezh***

■ **YOU MAY HEAR**

Plačajte pri blagajni
***pla**-cha^y-te pree bla-**ga^y**-nee*
Pay at the till

■ **MONEY** ■ **SHOPPING**

69

Unleaded petrol is widely available. Petrol stations on main roads are usually open 24 hours.

SUPER	SUPER
UNLEADED	NEOSVINČENI BENCIN
DIESEL	DIESEL

Where is there a petrol station?
Kje je bencinska črpalka?
*kⁱe ye ben-**tseen**-ska chrr-**pal**-ka*

Fill it up, please
Polno, prosim
*po**ʷ**-no pro-seem*

Please check the oil
Prosim, preverite olje
*pro-seem pre-**ve**-ree-te **ol**-ye*

Please check the tyre pressure
Prosim, preverite pritisk v zračnicah
*pro-seem pre-**ve**-ree-te pree-**teesk** oo **zrach**-nee-tsa-h*

Please clean the windscreen
Prosim, očistite mi vetrobransko steklo
*pro-seem o-**chee**-stee-te mee vet-ro-**bran**-sko **stek**-lo*

Do you have distilled water?
Imate destilirano vodo?
*ee-**ma**-te des-tee-**lee**-ra-no **vo**-do*

■ YOU MAY HEAR

Koliko bencina želite
***ko**-lee-ko ben-**tsee**-na zhe-**lee**-te*
How much petrol do you want?

Mislim, da imate premalo olja
***mees**-leem da ee-**ma**-te pre-**ma**-lo **ol**-ya*
I think the oil is a bit low

■ BREAKDOWNS ■ CAR

PHARMACY	LEKARNA
PRESCRIPTION	RECEPT
CHEMIST ON DUTY	DEŽURNA LEKARNA

Where is the nearest chemist?
Kje je najbližja lekarna?
kYe ye naY-bleezh-ya le-kar-na

I'd like something for...
Rad(a) bi nekaj proti...
rad(a) bee ne-kaY pro-tee...

a headache
glavobolu
gla-vo-bo-loo

diarrhoea
driski
dree-skee

travel sickness
potovalna slabost
po-to-val-na sla-bost

I have indigestion
Imam prebavne motnje
ee-mam pre-baw-ne mot-nYe

Is it safe to give to children?
Je to primerno za otroke?
ye to pree-meer-no za o-tro-ke

■ YOU MAY HEAR

Dvakrat...	Trikrat...	na dan
dva-krat...	**tree**-krat...	na dan
Twice...	Three times...	a day

■ WORDS YOU MAY NEED

antiseptic	razkužilo	raz-koo-**zhee**-lo
condoms	kondomi	kon-**do**-mee
cotton wool	vata	**va**-ta
plasters	povoji	po-**vo**-yee
sanitary pads	higienski vložki	hee-gee-**en**-skee **vlozh**-kee
tampons	tamponi	tam-**po**-nee

■ BODY ■ DOCTOR

71

Films can be bought at photographic shops, gift shops and at some supermarkets, but not at pharmacies.

Where can I buy tapes for a camcorder?
Kje lahko kupim kasete za video rekorder?
k^ye la-**hko koo**-peem ka-**se**-te za **vee**-de-o re-**kor**-der

I'd like a film for this camera
Rad(a) bi film za fotoaparat
rad(a) bee feelm za **fo**-to-a-pa-rat

a colour film	**a black and white film**
barvni film	črno beli film
barv-nee feelm	**chrr**-no **be**-lee feelm

with 24 exposures
s štiriindvajsetimi posnetki
s-**shtee**-ree-een-dva^y-se-tee-mee pos-**net**-kee

Can you develop this film?
Lahko razvijete ta film?
la-**hko** raz-**vee**-ye-te ta feelm

How long will it take?
Kako dolgo bo trajalo?
ka-**ko** do^w-go bo **tra**-ya-lo

Is it OK to take a photo of this?
Lahko to fotografiram?
la-**hko** to fo-to-gra-**fee**-ram

Can you take a photo of us, please?
Bi nas prosim slikali?
bee nas pro-seem **slee**-ka-lee

■ YOU MAY HEAR

Tukaj je prepovedano fotografirati
too-ka^y ye pre-po-**ve**-da-no fo-to-gra-**fee**-ra-tee
You can't take photos here

A first and second class service does not exist. For a quicker service ask for ekspres *. Tell the assistant where you are sending things to, as rates vary from country to country. Stamps for postcards are cheaper. Post offices are open 0800-1800 Mon.-Fri., 0800-1200 on Saturdays. Phonecards can also be bought at post offices. Stamps are also available at newsstands and other authorized sellers. Postboxes are yellow.*

POST OFFICE	POŠTA	POST CARD	RAZGLEDNICA
LETTER	PISMO	STAMPS	ZNAMKE

Where is the post office?
Kje je pošta?
k^ye ye **posh**-ta

Is it open?
Je odprta?
ye od-**prr**-ta

10 stamps
Deset znamk
de-**set** znamk

for postcards
za razglednice
za raz-**gled**-nee-tse

to Europe
za Evropo
za e^w-**ro**-po

to America
za Ameriko
za a-**me**-ree-ko

to Australia
za Avstralijo
za a^w-**stra**-lee-yo

a phonecard
Telefonska kartica
te-le-**fon**-ska **kar**-tee-tsa

Where can I post...?
Kje lahko oddam...?
k^ye la-**hko** od-**dam**...?

this letter
to pismo
to **pee**-smo

this postcard
to razglednico
to raz-**gled**-nee-tso

I want to send this... *(man)*
To bi rad poslal...
to bee rad pos-**la**^w...

(woman)
To bi rada poslala...
to bee **ra**-da pos-**la**-la...

registered
priporočeno
pree-po-**ro**-che-no

express
ekspres
ex-**pres**

■ YOU MAY HEAR

Pošta je danes zaprta
posh-ta ye **da**-nes za-**prr**-ta
The post office is closed today

■ NUMBERS ■ PAYING

73

Can you help me?
Mi lahko pomagate?
mee la-__hko__ po-__ma__-ga-te

I don't speak Slovene well
Ne govorim dobro slovensko
ne go-vo-__reem do__-bro slo-__ven__-sko

Does anyone here speak English?
Ali tukaj kdo govori angleško?
a-lee __too__-ka^y kdo go-vo-__ree__ an-__glesh__-ko

I've lost my... *(man)*
Izgubil sem...
eez-__goo__-bee^w sem...

(woman)
Izgubila sem...
eez-goo-__bee__-la sem...

	passport	money
	potni list	denar
	__pot__-nee leest	de-__nar__

I'm lost *(man)*
Izgubil sem se
eez-__goo__-bee^w sem se

(woman)
Izgubila sem se
eez-goo-__bee__-la sem se

I missed my... *(man)*
Zamudil sem...
za-__moo__-dee^w sem...

(woman)
Zamudila sem...
za-__moo__-dee-la sem...

	train	plane
	vlak	letalo
	vlak	le-__ta__-lo

I need to go to the British Embassy
Moram iti na ambasado Velike Britanije
__mo__-ram __ee__-tee na am-ba-__sa__-do ve-__lee__-ke bree-__ta__-nee-ye

Leave me alone
Pustite me pri miru
poo-__stee__-te me pree __mee__-roo

I left my ... here *(man)*
Tukaj sem pozabil...
__too__-ka^y sem po-za-__bee__^w...

(woman)
Tukaj sem pozabila...
__too__-ka^y sem po-za-__bee__-la...

	sunglasses	camera
	sončna očala	fotoaparat
	__son__-chna o-__cha__-la	__fo__-to-a-pa-rat

■ **COMPLAINTS** ■ **EMERGENCIES**

When you approach a stranger and ask a question, it is polite to start with **oprostite...** *(excuse me) followed by your question.*

Do you have...?
  Imate...?
  *ee-**ma**-te...*

When...?
  Kdaj...?
  kdaʸ...

At what time...?
  Ob kateri uri...?
  *ob ka-**tee**-ree **oo**-ree...*

What time is it?
  Koliko je ura?
  *ko-lee-ko ye **oo**-ra*

Where is... / are...?
  Kje je... / so...?
  kʸe ye... / so...

Can I / we...?
  Lahko...?
  *la-**hko**...*

Is it... / Are they...?
  Ali je... / Ali so...?
  a-lee ye... / a-lee so...

Which one...?
  Kateri...?
  *ka-**tee**-ree...*

How far is...?
  Kako daleč je...?
  *ka-**ko da**-lech ye...*

Who...?
  Kdo...?
  kdo...

Who are you?
  Kdo ste vi?
  kdo ste vee

What...?
  Kaj...?
  kaʸ...

Why...?
  Zakaj...?
  *za-**kaʸ**...*

How much is it?
  Koliko stane?
  *ko-lee-ko **sta**-ne*

How much/many...?
  Koliko...?
  ko-lee-ko...

How...? / Pardon?
  Kako...?
  *ka-**ko**...*

What kind of...?
  Kakšen...?
  ***kak**-shen...*

Where are the toilets?
  Kje so toaletni prostori?
  *kʸe so to-a-**let**-nee pro-**sto**-ree*

■ **BASICS**

75

This is broken
 To je pokvarjeno
 *to ye pok-**var**-ye-no*

Where can I have this repaired?
 Kje bi mi lahko to popravili?
 *kჼe bee mee la-**hko** to po-**pra**-vee-lee*

My watch is broken
 Moja ura je pokvarjena
 ***mo**-ya **oo**-ra ye pok-**var**-ye-na*

These shoes need mending
 Ti čevlji so potrebni popravila
 *tee **chev**-lyee so po-**treb**-nee po-pra-**vee**-la*

How much will it be?
 Koliko bo stalo?
 ***ko**-lee-ko bo **sta**-lo*

Can you do it straightaway?
 Lahko to naredite takoj?
 *la-**hko** to na-re-**dee**-te ta-**koy***

How long will the repairs take?
 Kako dolgo bo trajalo popravilo?
 *ka-**ko** doᵂ-go bo **tra**-ya-lo po-pra-**vee**-lo*

When will it be ready?
 Kdaj bo gotovo?
 *kdaჼ bo go-**to**-vo*

When will they be ready?
 Kdaj bodo gotovi?
 *kdaჼ **bo**-do go-**to**-vee*

The light bulb has gone
 Žarnica je pregorela
 ***zhar**-nee-tsa ye pre-go-**re**-la*

The ... doesn't work
 ...ne deluje
 *....ne de-**loo**-ye*

The washbasin is blocked
 Umivalnik je zamašen
 *oo-mee-**val**-neek ye za-ma-**shen***

■ **YOU MAY HEAR**

To se ne da popraviti
 *to se ne da po-**pra**-vee-tee*
This can't be mended

■ **BREAKDOWNS**

ROOM SERVICE	POSTREŽBA V SOBI
ROOM MAID	SOBARICA

Come in!   **Please come back later!**
Naprej!   Prosim, pridite kasneje!
na-**prey**   pro-seem **pree**-dee-te kas-**ne**-ye

Please bring ... to my room
Prosim, prinesite mi ... v sobo
pro-seem pree-**ne**-see-te mee ... oo **so**-bo

breakfast	**a sandwich**	**toilet paper**
zajtrk	sendvič	toaletni papir
za**y**-trrk	**send**-veech	to-a-**let**-nee pa-**peer**

Can I have... (man)	**an iron**	**another blanket**
Bi lahko dobil...	likalnik	še eno odejo
bee la-**hko** do-**bee**ʷ...	lee-**kal**-neek	she **e**-no o-**de**-yo

Can I have... (woman)	**another towel**	**another hanger**
Bi lahko dobila...	še eno brisačo	še en obešalnik
bee la-**hko** do-**bee**-la...	she **e**-no bree-**sa**-cho	she en o-be-**shal**-neek

My room number is...
Številka moje sobe je...
shte-**veel**-ka **mo**-ye **so**-be ye...

Could I have my clothes washed and ironed?
Bi mi lahko oprali in zlikali obleko?
bee mee la-**hko** o-**pra**-lee een **zlee**-ka-lee o-**ble**-ko

Please order a taxi for me
Bi mi prosim naročili taxi
bee mee pro-seem na-ro-**chee**-lee **tak**-see

Please wake me at...
Zbudite me, prosim, ob...
zboo-**dee**-te me pro-seem ob...

■ HOTEL DESK ■ TELEPHONE

OPEN	ODPRTO
CLOSED	ZAPRTO
DEPARTMENT	ODDELEK
ESCALATOR	PREMIČNE STOPNIČE
SALE	RAZPRODAJA
DISCOUNT	ZNIŽANO
SPECIAL OFFER	POSEBNA PONUDBA

Where is the shopping centre?
Kje je nakupovalni center?
*kᵛe ye na-koo-po-**val**-nee **tsen**-ter*

Where can I buy...?
Kje lahko kupim...?
*kᵛe la-**hko** koo-peem...*

gifts
darila
*da-**ree**-la*

souvenirs
spominke
*spo-**meen**-ke*

I'm looking for a present...
Iščem darilo...
*eesh-chem da-**ree**-lo...*

for my mother
za svojo mamo
*za **svo**-yo **ma**-mo*

for a child
za otroka
*za o-**tro**-ka*

Do you have anything...?
Imate kaj...?
*ee-**ma**-te kaᵛ...*

larger
večjega
***vech**-ye-ga*

smaller
manjšega
***man**ᵛ-sheg-a*

Could you show me something else, please?
Mi lahko pokažete še kaj drugega, prosim?
*mee la-**hko** po-**ka**-zhe-te she kaᵛ **droo**-ge-ga pro-seem*

This is too expensive
To je predrago
*to ye pred-**ra**-go*

Where is the market?
Kje je tržnica?
*kᵛe ye **trrzh**-nee-tsa*

■ YOU MAY HEAR

Želite, prosim?
*zhe-**lee**-te pro-seem*
May I help you?

Še kaj drugega?
*she kaᵛ **droo**-ge-ga*
Anything else?

Shops open from 0730 until 1900 during the week and from 0730 to 1300 on Saturdays.

baker's pekarna *pe-**kar**-na*

bookshop knjigarna *knyee-**gar**-na*

butcher mesnica *mes-**nee**-tsa*

cake shop slaščičarna *slash-chee-**char**-na*

clothes shop trgovina z obleko *trr-go-**vee**-na z o-**ble**-ko*

delicatessen delikatesa *de-lee-ka-**te**-sa*

DIY napravi si sam *na-**pra**-vee see sam*

dry-cleaner's čistilnica *chee-**steel**-nee-tsa*

electrical goods električni aparati *e-**lek**-treech-nee a-pa-**ra**-tee*

fishmonger's ribarnica *ree-**bar**-nee-tsa*

florist cvetličarna *tsvet-lee-**char**-na*

fruit shop trgovina s sadjem *trr-go-**vee**-na s **sad**-yem*

furniture trgovina s pohištvom *trr-go-**vee**-na s po-heesht-vom*

gifts spominki *spo-**meen**-kee*

grocer's špecerijska trgovina *shpe-tse-**reey**-ska trr-go-**vee**-na*

hairdresser's frizer *free-**zer***

jeweller's zlatarna *zla-**tar**-na*

market tržnica *trrzh-nee-tsa*

newsagent prodajalna časopisov *pro-da-**yal**-na cha-so-**pee**-sov*

optician optik *op-teek*

perfume shop parfumerija *par-foo-me-**ree**-ya*

pharmacy lekarna *le-**kar**-na*

photographic shop fotograf *fo-to-**graf***

shoe shop trgovina s čevlji *trr-go-**vee**-na s **chev**-lyee*

stationer's papirnica *pa-**peer**-nee-tsa*

supermarket supermarket *soo-per-mar-ket*

tobacconist's trafika *tra-**fee**-ka*

toyshop trgovina z igračami *trr-go-**vee**-na z ee-**gra**-cha-mee*

Where is the tourist office?
Kje je turistična agencija?
k^ye ye too-**ree**-steech-na a-gen-**tsee**-ya

What is there to see here?
Kaj si lahko ogledamo?
ka^y see la-**hko** o-**gle**-da-mo

Have you any brochures?
Imate brošure?
ee-**ma**-te bro-**shoo**-re

Do you have a programme of events?
Imate program prireditev?
ee-**ma**-te pro-**gram** pree-re-**dee**-te^w

What time is the sightseeing tour?
Ob kateri uri so ogledi mesta?
ob ka-**tee**-ree **oo**-ree so o-**gle**-dee **mes**-ta

How much is the guided tour?
Koliko stane ogled z vodičem?
ko-lee-ko **sta**-ne o-**gled** z vo-**dee**-chem

How do I get to...
Kako pridem v...
ka-**ko** pree-dem oo...

the old part of town
stari del mesta
sta-ree de^w **mes**-ta

When does the ... open?
Kdaj odprejo...?
kda^y od-**pre**-yo...

the museum
muzej
moo-**zey**

How much is the entrance fee to...?
Koliko stane vstopnina v...?
ko-lee-ko **sta**-ne ^wstop-**nee**-na oo...

gallery
galerijo
ga-le-**ree**-yo

castle	**monastery**	**town hall**
grad	samostan	rotovž
grad	sa-mo-**stan**	rot-o^wzh

Are there reductions...?	**for students**	**for children**
Ali je popust...?	za študente	za otroke
a-lee ye po-**poost**...	za shtoo-**den**-te	za o-**tro**-ke

■ **MAPS, GUIDES & NEWSPAPERS**

BLAGAJNA	CASH DESK
DVIGALO	LIFT
IZHOD	EXIT
KADILCI	SMOKING
KADITI PREPOVEDANO	NO SMOKING
MOŠKI	GENTS
NE DELUJE	OUT OF ORDER
NEKADILCI	NO SMOKING
ODDAJAMO SOBE	ROOMS TO LET
ODHOD	DEPARTURE
ODPRTO	OPEN
ODPRTO OD…DO…	OPEN FROM…UNTIL…
PARKIRANJE PREPOVEDANO	NO PARKING
PITNA VODA	DRINKING WATER
POTEGNI	PULL
POZVONI	RING THE BELL
PREPOVEDANO…	…FORBIDDEN / NO…
PRIHOD	ARRIVAL
PRITLIČJE	BASEMENT
PRIVAT	PRIVATE
PROSTO	FREE / VACANT
RAZPRODAJA	SALE
RINI	PUSH
VSTOP	ENTRANCE
VSTOP PROST	ENTRANCE FREE
VSTOP PREPOVEDAN	NO ENTRANCE
VSTOPNICE	TICKETS
ZAPRTO	CLOSED
ZASEDENO	ENGAGED / FULL
ZASILNI IZHOD	EMERGENCY EXIT
ŽENSKE	LADIES

SKIING	ALPSKO SMUČANJE
CROSS-COUNTRY SKIING	TEK NA SMUČEH
BEGINNERS	ZAČETNIKI
ADVANCED	IZKUŠENI SMUČARJI
SKI LIFT	SMUČARSKA ŽIČNICA

I'd like to hire skis (man)
Rad bi najel smuči
*rad bee na-ye***w** *smoo-chee*

(woman)
Rada bi najela smuči
ra-da bee na-ye-la smoo-chee

Does the price include...?
Ali so v ceno vključeni...?
a-lee so oo tse-no **w***klyoo-che-nee...*

ski boots
smučarski čevlji
smoo-char-skee che***w***-lyee

ski bindings
smučarske vezi
smoo-char-ske ve-**zee**

ski poles
smučarske palice
smoo-char-ske pa-lee-tse

How much is a ... pass?
Koliko stane ... karta?
ko-lee-ko **sta**-ne ... **kar**-ta

daily
dnevna
dne*w*-na

weekly
tedenska
te-den-ska

Do you have a map of the pistes?
Imate zemljevid smučarskih stez?
*ee-**ma**-te zem-l*y*e-**veed** smoo-char-sheeh stez*

Is there a skiing course?
Je na voljo smučarski tečaj?
*ye na **vol**-yo **smoo**-char-skee te-cha*y

Is there a skiing instructor here?
Je tukaj na voljo smučarski učitelj?
*ye **too**-ka*y *na **vol**-yo **smoo**-char-skee oo-**chee**-tel*y

■ YOU MAY HEAR

Ste prvič na smučeh?
*ste **prr**-veech na smoo-**che**-h*
Is it your first time skiing?

Where can we go...?
Kam bi lahko šli...?
*kam bee la-**hko** shlee...*

I'd like to hire... *(man)*
Rad bi najel...
*rad bee na-**ye**ʷ...*

I'd like to hire... *(woman)*
Rada bi najela...
*ra-da bee na-**ye**-la*

fishing
lovit ribe
*lo-**veet** ree-be*

riding
jahat
ya-hat

a mountain bike and helmet
gorsko kolo in čelado
gor-sko ko-lo een che-la-do

golf clubs
opremo za golf
*o-**pre**-mo za golf*

tennis equipment
opremo za tenis
*o-**pre**-mo za te-nees*

water-skis
vodne smuči
vod-ne smoo-chee

a boat
čoln
choʷn

a deckchair
ležalnik
*le-**zhal**-neek*

How much is it...?
Koliko stane...?
ko-lee-ko sta-ne...

per hour
na uro
na oo-ro

per day
na dan
na dan

per week
na teden
na ted-en

I'd like to go riding *(man)*
Rad bi jahal konja
rad bee ya-haʷ kon-ya

(woman)
Rada bi jahala konja
ra-da bee ya-ha-la kon-ya

Where can I buy a fishing licence?
Kje lahko kupim dovoljenje za ribolov?
kʸe la-hko koo-peem do-vol-yen-ye za ree-bo-loʷ

Are you a member of any sports club?
Ali ste član kakšnega športnega društva?
a-lee ste chlan kak-shne-ga shport-ne-ga droosht-va

Do you like playing...?
Ali radi igrate...?
*a-lee **ra**-dee ee-**gra**-te...*

football
nogomet
***no**-go-met*

basketball
košarko
*ko-**shar**-ko*

badminton
badminton
***bad**-meen-ton*

golf
golf
golf

netball
odbojko
*od-**boy**-ko*

handball
rokomet
***ro**-ko-met*

tennis
tenis
***te**-nees*

I like...
Rad(a)...
rad(a)...

swimming
plavam
***pla**-vam*

fishing
lovim ribe
*lo-**veem ree**-be*

cycling
kolesarim
*ko-le-**sa**-reem*

Where is the sports centre?
Kje je športni center?
*k^ye ye **shport**-nee **tsen**-ter*

Is it safe to swim here?
Je tu varno plavati?
*ye too **var**-no **pla**-va-tee*

Where is a swimming pool?
Kje je kopališče?
*k^ye ye ko-pa-**leesh**-che*

Is there a tennis coach available?
Je na voljo tenis učitelj?
*ye na **vol**-yo **te**-nees u-**chee**-tel^y*

Is it safe for children?
Je varno za otroke?
*ye **var**-no za o-**tro**-ke*

■ **HIKING**

*Taxis are available in all larger towns, at the airports and at
railway stations. They are metered but it is advisable to ask how
much the fare will be, especially for longer journeys.*

Where is the taxi stand?
Kje je postajališče taksijev?
*kʸe ye po-sta-ya-**leesh**-che **tak**-see-yeʷ*

Could you call me a taxi, please?
Bi mi prosim poklicali taxi?
*bee mee pro-**seem** po-**klee**-tsa-lee **tak**-see*

Please take me...
Bi me prosim peljali...
*bee me pro-seem pel-**ya**-lee...*

to the train station
na železniško postajo
*na zhe-**lez**-neesh-ko po-**sta**-yo*

to the airport
na letališče
*na le-ta-**leesh**-che*

to hotel...
v hotel...
*oo ho-**tel**...*

to the centre
v center mesta
*oo tsen-ter **mes**-ta*

to this address
na ta naslov
*na ta na-**sloʷ***

How much will it be?
Koliko bo stala vožnja?
***ko**-lee-ko bo **sta**-la **vozh**-nya*

I'm in a hurry
Mudi se mi
*moo-**dee** se mee*

How far is it to...?
Kako daleč je do...?
*ka-**ko da**-lech ye do...*

Please stop here
Prosim, ustavite tukaj
*pro-seem oo-**sta**-vee-te **too**-kaʸ*

Can you wait for me?
Bi me prosim počakali?
*bee me pro-seem po-**cha**-ka-lee*

Keep the change
Obdržite drobiž
*Ob-**drr**-zhee-te dro-**beezh***

■ **BUS**

The international code for Slovenia is 00 386 plus the town or area code less the first 0, e.g. Ljubljana (0)61, Maribor (0)62. In Slovenia you can make phone calls from post offices or from phone boxes. At the post office you pay for your call at the counter, whilst street phones take phonecards or tokens, both of which you can buy at post offices or at newsstands.

TELEPHONE BOX	TELEFONSKA KABINA
TELEPHONE DIRECTORY	TELEFONSKI IMENIK
PHONECARD	TELEFONSKA KARTICA
TELEPHONE TOKEN	ŽETON ZA TELEFON

I'd like to make a phone call *(man)*   *(woman)*
  Rad bi telefoniral   Rada bi telefonirala
  *rad be te-le-fo-**nee**-ra^w*   **ra**-da bee te-le-fo-**nee**-ra-la

Can I make a phone call from here?
  Ali lahko od tukaj telefoniram?
  *a-lee la-**hko** od **too**-kaY te-le-fo-**nee**-ram*

Please show me...   **how this phone works**
  Bi mi prosim pokazali...   kako deluje ta telefon
  *bee mee pro-seem po-**ka**-za-lee...*   *ka-**ko** de-**loo**-ye ta te-le-**fon***

How can I get an outside line?
  Kako dobim zvezo?
  *ka-ko do-**beem** zve-zo*

Has this telephone a direct line?
  Ima ta telefon direktno linijo?
  *ee-**ma** ta te-le-**fon** dee-**rekt**-no **lee**-nee-yo*

Where can I buy...? **telephone tokens** **a phonecard**
  Kje lahko kupim...?   žetone za telefon   telefonsko kartico
  *kYe la-**hko** koo-peem...* *zhe-**to**-ne za te-le-**fon*** *te-le-**fon**-sko **kar**-tee-tso*

Hello?   **Who is speaking?**
  Prosim?   Kdo je pri telefonu?
  pro-seem   *kdo ye pree te-le-**fo**-noo*

Extension...
  Interno...
  *een-**ter**-no...*

I'd like to speak to... *(man)*   *(woman)*
  Rad bi govoril z...   Rada bi govorila z...
  *rad bee go-vo-**ree**ʷ z...*   *ra-da bee go-vo-**ree**-la z...*

This is Mr... / Mrs...
  Gospod... / Gospa... pri telefonu
  *gos-**pod**... / gos-**pa**... pree te-le-**fo**-noo*

I'll call back... *(man)*   *(woman)*
  Poklical(a) bom...   Poklicala bom...
  *pok-**lee**-tsaʷ bom...*   *pok-**lee**-tsa-la bom...*

later	**tomorrow**
kasneje	jutri
*ka-**sne**-ye*	***yoo**-tree*

When will he/she be back?   **When should I call?**
  Kdaj pride nazaj?   Kdaj naj pokličem?
  *kdaʸ **pree**-de na-**za**ʸ*   *kdaʸ naʸ po-**klee**-chem*

■ YOU MAY HEAR

Prosim?   **Kdo je pri telefonu?**
  pro-seem   *kdo ye pree te-le-**fo**-noo*
  Hello?   **Who is speaking**

Trenutek, prosim
  *tre-**noo**-tek pro-seem*
  Just a moment

Zasedeno je   **Poskusite malo kasneje**
  *za-**se**-de-no ye*   *po-**skoo**-see-te **ma**-lo ka-**sne**-ye*
  The line is engaged   **Try a bit later**

Želite pustiti sporočilo?
  *zhe-**lee**-te poos-**tee**-tee spo-ro-**chee**-lo*
  Do you want to leave a message?

■ BUSINESS ■ FAX ■ OFFICE

SION PROGRAMME	TV SPORED
REMOTE CONTROL	DALJINSKI UPRAVJALEK
SERIES	SERIJA
SOAP OPERA	SENTIMENTALNA IGRA
CARTOONS	RISANKE
NEWS	POROČILA

What's on television?
Kaj je na televizijskem programu?
*ka^y ye na te-le-**vee**-zeey-skem pro-**gra**-moo*

How do I switch it on?
Kako ga prižgem?
*ka-ko ga preezh-**gem***

How do I switch it off?
Kako ga ugasnem?
*ka-ko ga oo-**gas**-nem*

When is the news?
Kdaj so poročila?
*kda^y so po-ro-**chee**-la*

Do you have any English language channels?
Ali obstaja kanal v angleškem jeziku?
*a-lee ob-**sta**-ya ka-na^w oo an-**glesh**-kem ye-**zee**-koo*

When are there any children's programmes?
Kdaj je kakšen otroški program?
*kda^y ye **kak**-shen o-**trosh**-kee pro-**gram***

Do you have any English videos?
Imate kakšen angleški video?
*ee-**ma**-te **kak**-shen an-**glesh**-kee **vee**-de-o*

What is your favourite programme?
Kateri je vaš najljubši program?
*ka-**tee**-ree ye vash na^y-**lyoob**-shee pro-**gram***

Please could you lower the volume
Znižajte glasnost, prosim
*znee-zha^y-te glas-**nost** pro-seem*

THEATRE	GLEDALIŠČE
OPERA	OPERA
STALLS	PARTER
DRESS CIRCLE	PRVI BALKON
UPPER CIRCLE	DRUGI BALKON
BOX	LOŽA
SEAT	SEDEŽ
CLOAKROOM	GARDEROBA

What's on at the theatre?
Kaj igra v gledališču?
ka^y ee-**gra** oo gle-da-**leesh**-choo

What's on at the opera?
Kaj igra v operi?
ka^y ee-**gra** oo **o**-pe-ree

How do we get to the theatre?
Kako bi prišli do gledališča?
ka-**ko** bee pree-**shlee** do gle-da-**leesh**-cha

How much are the tickets?
Koliko stanejo karte?
ko-lee-ko **sta**-ne-yo **kar**-te

2 tickets for...
Dve karti za...
dve **kar**-tee za...

tonight
danes zvečer
da-nes zve-**cheer**

tomorrow night
jutri zvečer
yoo-tree zve-**cheer**

When does the performance begin?
Ob kateri uri se začne predstava?
ob ka-**tee**-ree **oo**-ree se zach-**ne** pred-**sta**-va

When does the performance end?
Ob kateri uri se konča predstava?
ob ka-**tee**-ree **oo**-ree se kon-**cha** pred-**sta**-va

I enjoyed the play
Igra mi je bila všeč
ee-gra mee ye bee-**la** ^wshech

I enjoyed the opera
Opera mi je bila všeč
o-per-a mee ye bee-**la** ^wshech

■ ENTERTAINMENT ■ MUSIC

The 24-hour clock is used on TV, radio, timetables, etc. The 12-hour clock is used in everyday speech but the many endings make it seem quite complicated. Ask someone to show you on their watch!

Excuse me!	**What time is it?**
Oprostite!	Koliko je ura?
*o-pro-**stee**-te*	*ko-lee-ko ye **oo**-ra*

It's...	**2 o'clock**	**5 o'clock**	**8 o'clock**
Ura je...	dve	pet	osem
***oo**-ra ye...*	*dve*	*pet*	***o**-sem*

half past 3 *(meaning half to 4)*
pol štirih
*po^w **shtee**-ree-h...*

quarter past 2 *(meaning three quarters onto 3)*
četrt na tri
*che-**trrt** na tree*

quarter to six *(meaning three quarters onto 6)*
tri četrt na šest
*tree che-**trrt** na shest*

7:30
sedem in trideset minut
sed**-em een **tree**-de-set mee-**noot

5:15
pet in petnajst minut
*pet een **pet**-na^yst mee-**noot***

9:45
devet in petinštirideset minut
*de-**vet** een **pet**-een-shtee-ree-de-set mee-**noot***

When is...?
Kdaj je...?
*kda*y *ye...*

When are...?
Kdaj so...?
*kda*y *so...*

Is it open?
Je odprto?
*ye od-**prr**-to*

Is it closed?
Je zaprto?
*ye za-**prr**-to*

When does it open?
Ob kateri uri se odpre?
*ob ka-**tee**-ree **oo**-ree se od-**pre***

When does it close?
Ob kateri uri se zapre?
*ob ka-**tee**-ree **oo**-ree se za-**pre***

When does it begin?
Ob kateri uri se začne?
*ob ka-**tee**-ree **oo**-ree se zach-**ne***

When does it finish?
Ob kateri uri se konča?
*ob ka-**tee**-ree **oo**-ree se kon-**cha***

at...	before...	after...
ob...	pred...	po...
ob...	*pred...*	*po...*

today	tonight	tomorrow	yesterday
danes	danes zvečer	jutri	včeraj
da-nes	*da*-nes zve-**cheer**	*yoo*-tree	wche-ra*y*

this morning	this afternoon	this evening
danes zjutraj	danes popoldne	danes zvečer
da-nes *zyoo*-tra*y*	*da*-nes po-**pow**d-ne	*da*-nes zve-**cheer**

in the morning	in the afternoon	in the evening
zjutraj	popoldne	zvečer
zyoo-tra*y*	po-**pow**d-ne	zve-**cheer**

in an hour's time	in half an hour	two hours ago
čez eno uro	čez pol ure	pred dvema urama
*chez **e**-no **oo**-ro*	*chez pow **oo**-re*	*pred **dve**-ma **oo**-ra-ma*

soon	early	late	later	too late
kmalu	zgodaj	pozno	pozneje	prepozno
kma-loo	**zgo**-da*y*	**poz**-no	poz-**ne**-ye	pre-**poz**-no

■ NUMBERS

SNACK BAR	BIFE
TRAIN	VLAK
TRAIN STATION	ŽELEZNIŠKA POSTAJA
PLATFORM	PERON
TIME TABLE	VOZNI RED
DELAY	ZAMUDA
LEFT LUGGAGE OFFICE	GARDEROBA
TICKET OFFICE	BLAGAJNA ZA PRODAJO VOZOVNIC
FIRST CLASS	PRVI RAZRED
SECOND CLASS	DRUGI RAZRED

Where is the station?
Kje je železniška postaja?
*k-ye je zhe-**lez**-neesh-ka po-**sta**-ya*

To the station, please
Na železniško postajo, prosim
*na zhe-**lez**-neesh-ko po-**sta**-yo pro-seem*

When is the next train to…?
Kdaj pelje naslednji vlak v…?
*kda^y **pel**-ye nas-**led**-nyee vlak v…*

I'd like…
Rad(a) bi…
rad(a) bee…

2 tickets
dve vozovnici
*dve vo-**zo^w**-nee-tsee*

single
enosmerno
***e**-no-smer-no*

return
povratno
*po^w-**rat**-no*

first class
za prvi razred
*za **prr**-vee **raz**-red*

second class
za drugi razred
*za **droo**-gee **raz**-red*

in smoking
v vagonu za kadilce
*v va-**go**-noo za ka-**deel**-tse*

in non-smoking
v vagonu za nekadilce
*v va-**go**-noo za **ne**-ka-**deel**-tse*

When is...?
 Kdaj pelje...?
 kda^y pel-ye...?

the first train to...
 prvi vlak v...
 prr-vee vlak oo...

the last train to...
 zadnji vlak v...
 zad-nyee vlak oo...

Will I have to change? *(man)*
 Bom moral prestopiti?
 bom mo-ra^w pres-to-pee-tee

(woman)
 Bom morala prestopiti?
 bom mo-ra-la pres-to-pee-tee

Where do I have to change?
 Kje moram prestopiti?
 k-ye mo-ram pres-to-pee-tee

Is this a direct train?
 Je to direkten vlak?
 ye to dee-rek-ten vlak

Does the train stop at...?
 Ali se vlak ustavi v...?
 a-lee se vlak oo-sta-vee v...

When does the train arrive in...?
 Kdaj prispe vlak v...
 kda^y prees-pe vlak v...

Please tell me when to get off
 Povejte mi prosim, kdaj naj izstopim
 po-vey-te mee pro-seem kda^y na^y eez-sto-peem

Where is the dining car?
 Kje je jedilni vagon?
 k-ye ye ye-deel-nee va-gon

Is this seat free?
 Je sedež prost?
 ye se-dezh prost

I have a reservation
 Imam rezervacijo
 ee-mam re-zer-va-tsee-yo

Excuse me!
 Oprostite!
 o-pro-stee-te

■ **LUGGAGE**

Are there any vegetarian restaurants?
Kje je kakšna vegetarijanska restavracija?
*k-ye ye **ka**-kshna ve-ge-ta-ree-**yan**-ska re-staᵂ-**ra**-tsee-ya*

What soups without meat do you have?
Katere brezmesne juhe imate?
*ka-**tee**-re **brez**-mes-ne **yoo**-he ee-**ma**-te*

What dishes without meat do you have?
Katere brezmesne jedi imate?
*ka-**tee**-re **brez**-mes-ne ye-**dee** ee-**ma**-te*

Where are the vegetarian dishes?
Kje so vegetarijanske jedi?
*k-ye so ve-ge-ta-ree-**yan**-ske ye-**dee***

I don't eat meat
Ne jem mesa
*ne yem me-**sa***

What do you recommend?
Kaj mi priporočate?
*kaʸ mee pree-po-**ro**-cha-te*

Is this cooked in vegetable oil?
Je to pripravljeno v rastlinskem olju?
*je to pree-**prav**-lʸe-no oo rast-**leen**-skem **ol**-yoo*

What salads do you have?
Kakšne solate imate?
***kak**-shne so-**la**-te ee-**ma**-te*

WEATHER FORECAST	VREMENSKA NAPOVED
CLEAR SKY	JASNO
SUNNY	SONČNO
CLOUDY	OBLAČNO
RAIN	DEŽ
SNOW	SNEG
SHOWERS	NEVIHTE

What a lovely day!
Kakšen lep dan!
kak-shen lep dan

What awful weather!
Kako grdo vreme!
ka-**ko grr**-do **vre**-me

It's sunny	**It's raining**	**It's snowing**	**It's windy**
Sončno je	Dežuje	Sneži	Verovno je
sonch-no ye	de-**zhoo**-ye	sne-**zhee**	ve-**tro**^w-no ye

What will the weather be like tomorrow?
Kakšno bo jutri vreme?
kak-shno bo **yoo**-tree **vre**-me

Do you think it's going to rain?
Ali mislite, da bo deževalo?
a-lee **mee**-slee-te da bo de-zhe-**va**-lo

Do I need an umbrella?
Ali potrebujem dežnik?
a-lee po-tre-**boo**-yem dezh-**neek**

It's very hot today
Danes je zelo vroče
da-nes ye ze-**lo vro**-che

It's very cold today
Danes je zelo mrzlo
da-nes ye ze-**lo mrr**-zlo

Does it snow here in the winter?
Ali tukaj pozimi sneži?
a-lee **too**-ka^y po-**zee**-mee sne-**zhee**

Is it hot in the summer?
Ali je poleti vroče?
a-lee ye po-**le**-tee **vro**-che

■ **MAKING FRIENDS**

WINE LIST	VINSKA KARTA
APERITIFS	APERITIVI
SPIRITS	ŽGANE PIJAČE

The wine list, please?
Vinsko karto, prosim?
*veen-sko **kar**-to pro-seem*

a bottle of...
steklenico...
*stek-le-**nee**-tso...*

please
prosim
pro-seem

white wine
belo vino
***be**-lo **vee**-no*

red wine
rdeče vino
*rr-**de**-che **vee**-no*

table wine
namizno vino
*na-**meez**-no **vee**-no*

local wine
domače vino
*do-**ma**-che **vee**-no*

dry wine
suho vino
***soo**-ho **vee**-no*

medium dry wine
polsuho vino
*po^w-soo-ho **vee**-no*

medium sweet wine
polsladko vino
*po^w-**slad**-ko **vee**-no*

sweet wine
sladko vino
***slad**-ko **vee**-no*

dessert wine
desertno vino
*de-**sert**-no **vee**-no*

rosé wine
rozé vino
*ro-**ze vee**-no*

wines made from selected overripe grapes
jagodni in suhi jagodni izbori
***ya**-god-nee een **soo**-hee **ya**-god-nee eez-**bo**-ree*

Could you recommend a good Slovene wine?
Bi nam lahko priporočili kakšno dobro slovensko vino?
*bee nam la-**hko** pree-po-**ro**-chee-lee **kak**-shno **do**-bro slo-ven-sko **vee**-no*

Is this very strong?
Je to zelo močno?
*ye to ze-**lo moch**-no*

I like spirits
Rad(a) imam žgane pijače
rad(a) ee-**mam zhga**-ne pee-**ya**-che

I don't like spirits
Nimam rad(a) žganih pijač
nee-mam rad(a) **zhga**-nee-h pee-**yach**

■ WINES & SPIRITS

Kraški teran	*strong, rich red wine made from grapes grown in the iron-bearing soil of the Karst region*
Refošk	*dense, almost violet-coloured red wine grown on the Slovenian coast*
Traminec	*semi-dry, spicy dry white wine made from grapes grown along the banks of the Drava river*
Cviček rosé	*a popular, tasty, dry rosé made from grapes grown in the Save valley*
Renski rizling	*dry white wine of medium quality*
Zlata radgonska penina	*sparkling white wine made according to the traditional Champagne method*
Slivovka	*plum brandy, Slivovitz.*

■ DRINKING ■ EATING OUT

What do you do for a living?
Kaj ste po poklicu?
*ka^y ste po pok-**lee**-tsoo*

Do you enjoy this work?
Vam je to delo všeč?
*vam ye to **de**-lo ʷshech*

I'm a...	**doctor**
Jaz sem...	zdravnik / zdravnica
yaz sem...	*zdrav-**neek** / zdrav-**nee**-tsa*

	manager
	direktor / direktorica
	*dee-**rek**-tor / dee-**rek**-to-ree-tsa*

I work in...	**a shop**	**a factory**	**an office**
Delam v...	trgovini	tovarni	pisarni
***de**-lam oo...*	*trr-go-**vee**-nee*	*to-**var**-nee*	*pee-**sar**-nee*

I work from 9 to 5
Delam od devetih do petih
***de**-lam od de-**ve**-tee-h do **pe**-tee-h*

from Monday to Friday
od ponedeljka do petka
*od po-ne-**del**ʲ-ka do **pet**-ka*

I'm unemployed
Nezaposlen(a) sem
***ne**-za-pos-len(a) sem*

It's very difficult to get a job at the moment
Trenutno je zelo težko dobiti službo
*tre-**noot**-no ye ze-**lo tezh**-ko do-**bee**-tee **sloozh**-bo*

NOUNS

Slovene nouns can be masculine, feminine or neuter.

Masculine nouns usually end in a consonant, e.g.

| dežnik | umbrella | umbrellas | dežniki |
| pulover | pullover | pullovers | puloverji |

Feminine nouns usually end in **a** *, e.g.*

| cesta | road | roads | ceste |
| hiša | house | houses | hiše |

Neuter nouns usually end in **o** *or* **e** *, e.g.*

| mesto | town | towns | mesta |
| dete | baby | babies | deteta |

Slovene has no definite article **the** *or indefinite article* **a, an**.

ADJECTIVES

Adjectives must agree with the noun they modify in gender, case and number: this means that they also get endings. Sometimes the ending is simply added to the masculine stem of the adjective (see example **lep** *below) and sometimes there is a slight change in the order of the letters when feminine and neuter endings are added (see example* **majhen** *below).*

| lep(-a/-o) | beautiful |
| majhen(-hna/-o) | small |

The most common adjectival endings are no ending for adjectives modifying masculine nouns, e.g.

| lep pulover | beautiful jumper |
| majhen pulover | small jumper |

a *ending for adjectives modifying feminine nouns, e.g.*

| lepa hiša | beautiful house |
| majhna hiša | small house |

o ending for adjectives modifying neuter nouns e.g.

lepo vreme	**beautiful weather**
majhno mesto	**small town**

Adjectives always go in front of the noun they qualify.

Words like **my**, **your**, **his**, **her**, *etc. also depend on the gender, case and number of the noun they accompany. For example:*

masculine	feminine	neuter	
moj	moja	moje	**my**
vaš	vaša	vaše	**your** (plural and polite)
tvoj	tvoja	tvoje	**your** (familiar)
njegov	njegova	njegovo	**his**
njen	njena	njeno	**her**
naš	naša	naše	**our**
njiov	njihova	njihovo	**their**

COMPARISON OF ADJECTIVES

The comparatives and the superlatives of adjectives are formed by adding suffixes or by putting the words bolj **more** *and* najbolj **most** *in front of the adjective. However, there are exceptions. Here are some useful examples:*

	more	most	
drag	dražji	najdražji	**expensive**
poceni	cenejši	najcenejši	**cheap**
lep	lepši	najlepši	**beautiful**
velik	večji	največji	**big, tall**
bel	bolj bel	najbolj bel	**white**

(All other colours form the comparative and the superlative with these words in front of them.)

DUAL FORM

Unlike most languages, in Slovene all nouns, verbs and pronouns have, in addition to singular and plural, the dual form. In English you use the plural when talking of more than one person or thing. In Slovene you use the dual form for 2 people or 2 things. The plural form refers to more than 2 items.

PERSONAL PRONOUNS

jaz	**I**
ti	**you**
on	**he**
ona	**she**
ono	**it**
midva	**we 2**
vidva	**you 2**
onadva	**they 2**
mi	**we**
vi	**you**
oni	**they**

In Slovene, personal pronouns are usually omitted before verbs, since the verb ending generally distinguishes the person. They are used when you want to stress the person or to establish the sex of a person, i.e. **he**, **she** *(if this in not clear from the context of the conversation).*

FORMS FOR ADDRESSING PEOPLE

There are two ways of addressing people in Slovene, depending on their age, how well you know them and how formal or informal the relationship is.

Vi **you** *plural is the polite form of address*

Ti **you** *singular is the familiar form of address*

CASES

Nouns, adjectives and pronouns decline in Slovene by adding suffixes (tags added to the ends of words). The endings vary according to the part they play in the setence. Consult a grammar for declension tables, but you should be understood using the nominative case.

Slovene has six cases, they are:

1. Nominative
2. Genitive
3. Dative
4. Accusative
5. Locative
6. Instrumental

In the dictionary section we give the nominative form for nouns and adjectives. You will see in the phrases that the endings may differ according to what function they play in the sentence.

VERBS

The infinitive of Slovene verbs usually ends in …ti and sometimes in …či ,e.g.

govoriti	**to speak**
teči	**to run**

The following is the present tense of some of the most important irregular verbs

BITI (TO BE)

(jaz) sem **I am**
(ti) si **you are**
(on, ona, ono) je **(s)he, it is**

(midva) sva **we 2 are**
(vidva) sta **you 2 are**
(onadva) sta **they 2 are**

(mi) smo **we are**
(vi) ste **you are**
(oni) so **they are**

IMETI (TO HAVE)

imam **I have**
imaš **you have**
ima **(s)he, it has**

imava **we 2 have**
imata **you 2 have**
imata **they 2 have**

imamo **we have**
imate **you have**
imajo **they have**

ITI (TO GO)

(jaz) grem **I go**
(ti) greš **you go**
(on, ona, ono) gre **(s)he, it goes**

(midva) greva **we 2 go**
(vidva) gresta **you 2 go**
(onadva) gresta **they 2 go**

(mi) gremo **we go**
(vi) greste **you go**
(oni) grejo **they go**

VEDETI (TO KNOW)

vem **I know**
veš **you know**
ve **(s)he, it knows**

veva **we 2 know**
vesta **you 2 know**
vesta **they 2 know**

vemo **we know**
veste **you know**
vejo **they know**

JESTI (TO EAT)		HOTETI (TO WANT)	
(jaz) jem	**I eat**	hočem	**I want**
(ti) ješ	**you eat**	hočeš	**you want**
(on, ona, ono) je	**(s)he, it eats**	hoče	**(s)he, it wants**
(midva) jeva	**we 2 eat**	hočeva	**we 2 want**
(vidva) jesta	**you 2 eat**	hočeta	**you 2 want**
(onadva) jesta	**they 2 eat**	hočeta	**they 2 want**
(mi) jemo	**we eat**	hočemo	**we want**
(vi) jeste	**you eat**	hočete	**you want**
(oni) jejo	**they eat**	hočejo	**they want**

IMPERATIVES

Special endings are also added to verbs to form the imperative form. Here are some useful examples:

familiar	polite	
POČAKAJ!	POČAKAJTE!	**wait!**
POGLEJ!	POGLEJTE!	**look!**
POSLUŠAJ!	POSLUŠAJTE!	**listen!**
PRIZNAJ!	PRIZNAJTE!	**admit!**
VPRAŠJ!	VPRAŠAJTE!	**ask!**
TELEFONIRAJ!	TELEFONIRAJTE!	**telephone!**

PAST TENSE

The past tense is formed with the present tense of the verb 'to be' and the 'participle in l'.
You get the 'participle in l' by dropping the -ti ending from the infinitive and adding these endings onto the stem:

-l for masculine ending   e.g. govoril (spoke), povedal (told)

-la for feminine ending   e.g. govorila, povedala

-lo for neuter ending   e.g. govorilo, povedalo

-li for plural ending   e.g. govorili, povedali

For example:

Vodič je govoril vso pot	**The guide spoke the whole way**
Povedali so mam veliko	**They told us a lot**

FUTURE TENSE

The future tense is formed with the future tense of the verb 'to be' and the participle in l'. The forms of the verb 'to be' in the future tense are:

singular	dual	plural
bom **I will**	bova **we 2 will**	bomo **we will**
boš **you will**	bosta **you 2 will**	boste **you will**
bo **(s)he,it will**	bosta **they 2 will**	bodo **they will**

Examples:

počakal te bom	**I'll wait for you**
vsi bomo prišli	**we'll all come**

ASKING QUESTIONS

Questions in Slovene are formed with the question word **ali** *in all tenses and for all persons.* **Ali** *is often omitted as it is taken as understood.*

(Ali) imate proste sobe?	**Do you have rooms available?**
(Ali) govorite angleško?	**Do you speak English?**

Questions are also asked with interrogative pronouns and adverbs. The following are among the most common:

Kdo?	**Who?**
Zakaj?	**Why?**
Kje?	**Where?**
Kam?	**Where to?**
Čigav?	**Whose?**
Kako?	**How?**

NEGATIVE STATEMENTS

Statements in the present tense are negated by putting **ne** *in front of the verb, for example:*

ne vem	**I don't know**
ne govori!	**Don't speak!** *(familiar)*
ne skrbite!	**Don't worry!** *(polite)*

DICTIONARY
ENGLISH-SLOVENE
SLOVENE-**ENGLISH**

a	**see GRAMMAR**
about: about 10 o'clock	okoli desetih
abroad *adj*	v tujini
accelerator	pospeševalec
accent	naglas
(pronunciation)	izgovorjava
accept	sprejeti
accident	nesreča
accommodation	prenočišče ; dom
account	račun ; faktura
accountant	računovodja (-dkinja)
accustomed	navajen(-a/-o)
ache *vb*	boleti
my head aches	glava me boli
my stomach aches	trebuh me boli
my tooth aches	zob me boli
acknowledge *vb*	priznati
adaptor	adaptor
add *vb*	dodati
address	naslov
my address	moj naslov
your address	vaš naslov
address book	beležka z naslovi
adhesive tape	lepilni trak
adjust *vb*	prilagoditi
admit *vb*	priznati
admission charge	vstopnina
adult: for adults	za odrasle
advance: in advance	v naprej
advertisement	reklama
after	po
after lunch	po kosilu
afternoon	popoldan

this afternoon	danes popoldne
in the afternoon	popoldne
tomorrow afternoon	jutri popoldne
again	še enkrat
against *prep*	proti
age	starost
agent	zastopnik (zastopnica)
agree *vb*	strinjati se
agreement	dogovor
AIDS	AIDS
air-conditioning	klimatska naprava
is there air-conditioning?	imate klimatsko napravo?
air mail	letalska pošta
airplane	letalo
airport	letališče
to the airport	na letališče
air ticket	letalska vozovnica
alarm	alarm
fire alarm	požarni alarm
alarm clock	budilka
alcoholic *adj*	alkoholičen(-čna/-o)
all	ves ; cel
allergic to…	alergičen(-na) na…
I'm allergic to…	alergičen(-na) sem na…
allergy	alergija
alley	aleja
allow *vb*	dovoliti
all right	v redu
almonds	mandelji
almost	skoraj
alone	sam(-a)
alpine	alpski(-a/-o)

already	že
also	tudi
always	vedno ; zmeraj
am	see GRAMMAR
ambulance	rešilni avto
America	Amerika
American	Američan(-ka)
amount	vsota
anaesthetic	narkotik
anchor	sidro
and	in
angry	jezen(-zna/-o)
anorak	dežni jopič
another	še eden
another beer, please	še eno pivo, prosim
answer *vb*	odgovoriti
answerphone	telefonska tajnica
antibiotic	antibiotik
antifreeze	proti zmrzovanju
antiques	starine
antiseptic *n*	razkužilo
any	kaj
have you any apples?	imate jabolka?
anybody	kdorkoli
anything	karkoli
apartment	apartma
aperitif	aperitiv
apples	jabolka
apple juice	jabolčni sok
appointment	zmenek
apricots	marelice
April	april

are	see GRAMMAR
arm	roka
arrange *vb*	organizirati
arrest *vb*	aretirati
arrival	prihod
arrive	priti ; prispeti
art gallery	umetnostna galerija
arthritis	vnetje sklepov
artichokes	artičoke
article	članek
ashtray	pepelnik
asparagus	beluš
aspirin	aspirin
assistance	pomoč
asthma	astma
at	pri ; ob ; v
at home	doma
at 8 o'clock	ob osmih
at once	takoj
at night	ponoči
attack *n*	napad
heart attack	srčni napad
attractive	privlačen(-čna/-o)
aubergine	melancana
auction *n*	licitacija ; dražba
August	avgust
aunt	teta
my aunt	moja teta
Australia	Avstralija
Australian	Avstralec (Avstralka)
author	avtor
automatic	avtomatičen(-čna/-o)

automatic car	avtomobil z avtomatiskimi prestavami
autumn	jesen
available	na razpolago
avalance	plaz
avoid	izogniti se
awful	strašen(-šna/-o)
baby	dete
baby food	hrana za otroka
baby-sitter	varuška
bachelor	samec
back *(of body)*	hrbet
backward	nazaj
bacon	slanina
bad	slab(-o/-a)
badge	značka
bag	torba
handbag	torbica
baggage	prtljaga
bail	poroštvo
bait	vaba
baker's	pekarna
balcony	balkon
bald *(person)*	plešast(-a)
bald tyre	zvožena guma
ball	žoga
banana	banana
band *(musical)*	skupina
bandage	obveza; povoj
bank	banka

bank account	bančni račun
bar	bar
barber	brivec
basket	koš ; košara
basketball	košarka
bath	kopel
to take a bath	kopati se v kopalnici
bathing cap	kopalna kapa
bathroom	kopalnica
with bathroom	s kopalnico
battery	baterija
be	**see GRAMMAR**
beach	plaža
beans	fižol
beautiful	lep(-a/-o)
because	zato ; zato ker
become	postati
bed	postelja
double bed	zakonska postelja
single bed	postelja za eno osebo
bedding	posteljnina
bedroom	spalnica
my bedroom	moja soba
bee	čebela
beef	govedina
beetroot	pesa
before: before breakfast	pred zajtrkom
begin	začeti
behind	za ; zadaj
believe	verjeti
bell (doorbell)	zvonec
below	pod ; spodaj

belt	pas
beside (next to)	zraven
beside the bank	zraven banke
best	najboljši(-a/-e)
better (than)	bolje (kot)
bicycle	kolo
big	velik(-a/-o)
bigger	večji(-čja/-e)
bike	kolo
mountain bike	gorsko kolo
bill	račun
bin (dustbin)	smetnjak
binoculars	daljnogled
bird	ptica
birth certificate	rojstni list
birthday	rojstni dan
happy birthday!	vse najboljše za rojstni dan
my birthday is on…	moj rojstni dan je…
birthday card	voščilnica
biscuits	piškoti
bit: a bit	malo
bite (insect)	pik
bitten: I was bitten by a wasp	osa me je pičila
bitter (taste)	grenek(-nka/-o)
black	črn(-a/-o)
blackcurrant	črni ribez
blanket	odeja
bleach	belilo
blind (person)	slep(-a)
blind n (for window)	žaluzija
blocked	zaprt(-a/-o) ; blokiran(-a/-o)
blood	kri

blood group	krvna skupina
blouse	bluza
blow-dry	posušiti s fenom
blue	moder(-dra/-o)
boat	čoln
boat house	čolnarna
boat trip	izlet z ladjo
boil *vb*	vreti
bone	kost
book *n*	knjiga
book *vb*	rezervirati
booking	rezervacija
booking office *(train)*	železniška blagajna
bookshop	knjigarna
boots	škornji
walking boots	planinski čevlji
border	meja
boring	dolgočasen(-sna/-o)
borrow	izposoditi si
boss	šef ; gospodar
both	oba
bottle	steklenica
a bottle of wine, please	steklenico vina, prosim
a bottle of water, please	steklenico vode, prosim
a half-bottle	pol steklenice
bottle opener	odpirač za steklenice
box	škatla
box office *(theatre)*	gledališka blagajna
boy	fant
boyfriend	fant
my boyfriend	moj fant
bra	nedrček

bracelet	zapestnica
brakes	zavore
branch (of tree)	veja
(of business, etc.)	podružnica
brand (make)	znamka
brandy	vinjak
plum brandy	slivovka
brave	pogumen(-mna/-o)
bread	kruh
brown bread	črni kruh
white bread	beli kruh
break	zlomiti ; razbiti
breakable	lomljiv(-a/-o)
breakdown (car)	okvara na motorju
(nervous)	živčni zlom
breakfast	zajtrk
when is breakfast?	kdaj je zajtrk?
breast (of chicken)	belo meso
(of woman)	prsi
breath	dih
bride	nevesta
bridge	most
briefcase	aktovka
bring	prinesti
Britain	Britanija
British	Britanec (Britanka)
brochure	brošura
broken	zlomljen(-a/-o)
broken down (car, etc)	pokvarjen(-a/-o)
broom	metla
brother	brat
my brother	moj brat

brown	rjav(-a/-o)
brush	krtača
bucket	vedro
buffet car *(train)*	jedilni vagon
build *vb*	graditi
building	stavba
bulb *(lightbulb)*	žarnica
bureau de change	menjalnica
burn *vb*	goreti
bus	avtobus
bus stop/station	avtobusna postaja
bus tokens	žetoni
10 bus tokens	deset žetonov
bus tour	izlet z avtobusom
business: on business	poslovno
business card	vizitika
busy	zaseden(-a/-o)
but	ampak
butcher's	mesnica
butter	maslo
butterfly	metulj
button	gumb
buy *vb*	kupiti
by: by bus	z autobusom
by car	z avtom
by train	z vlakom
by ship	z ladjo
bye!	adijo!
bypass	obvoz

cab *(taxi)*	taksi
cabbage	zelje
cablecar	gondolska žičnica
café	kavarna
cake	torta
cake shop	slaščičarna
calendar	koledar
call *vb*	klicati ; poklicati
(phone)	telefonirati
calm	miren(-rna/-o)
camcorder	video rekorder
camera	fotoaparat
camp *vb*	kampirati
camping gas	plin
camping stove	kuhalnik
campsite	kamping
can *vb* : **can I...?**	lahko...?
I cannot...	ne morem...
can we...?	lahko...?
we cannot...	ne moremo
can *n*	pločevinka ; konzerva
Canada	Kanada
Canadian	Kanadčan (Kanadčanka)
cancel	odpovedati
candle	sveča
canoe	kanu
can opener	odpirač za konzerve
capital *(city)*	glavno mesto
car	avto
car hire	najeti avto
car keys	ključi od avta
my car keys	moji ključi od avta

carafe	karafa
caravan	prikolica
card (business)	vizitka
birthday card	voščilnica
Christmas card	božična voščilnica
cards (playing cards)	karte
careful	previden(-dna/-o)
carnation	nagelj
car ferry	trajekt
car park	parkirišče
carpet	preproga
carriage (railway)	vagon
carrots	korenje
carry	nesti ; nositi
car wash	avtopralnica
case (suitcase)	kovček
cash n	gotovina
cash vb	vnovčiti
cash desk	blagajna
cash point	bančni avtomat
casino	igralnica
cassette	kaseta
cassette recorder	kasetofon
castle	grad
casualty department	urgentni oddelek
cat	maček
cathedral	stolnica
cauliflower	cvetača
cave	jama
cd	CD
cd player	CD
ceiling	strop

celery	zélena
cemetery	pokopališče
centimetre	centimeter
central	osrednji(-a/-e)
central heating	centralna kurjava
centre	središče
town centre	središče mesta
century	stoletje
certificate	spričevalo
birth certificate	rojstni list
chain	veriga
chair	stol
champagne	šampanjec
chambermaid	sobarica
change *n (small coins)*	drobiž
change *vb (money)*	zamenjati
(change clothes)	preobleči se
(change bus/train)	prestopiti
changing room	kabina za preoblačenje
chapel	kapela
charge *n*	cena
cheap	poceni
cheaper	ceneje
check point	kontrola
check *vb*	kontrolirati
check-in *n*	prijava
cheerful	vesel(-a/-o) ; veder(-dra/-o)
cheers!	na zdravje!
cheese	sir
chemist's	lekarna
cheque	ček
cheque book	čekovna knjižica

cherries	češnje
chestnuts	kostanji
chicken	piščanec ; kura
chickenpox	norice
child	otrok
children	otroci
for children	za otroke
chilli	huda paprika
chips	pomes frittes
chocolate	čokolada
hot chocolate	kakav
chocolates	čokoladni bomboni
chop *(meat)*	zrezek
Christmas	božič
Merry Christmas!	vesel božič!
Christmas card	božična voščilnica
Christmas Eve	božični večer
church	cerkev
cider	jabolčnik
cigar	cigara
cigarette lighter	vžigalnik
cigarettes	cigarete
cinema	kino
circus	cirkus
city	mesto
city centre	središče mesta
class: first class	prvi razred
second class	drugi razred
clean *adj*	čist(-a/-o)
clean *vb*	čistiti
clear *adj*	jasen(-sna/-o)
client	stranka

climb vb	plezati
climbing boots	planinski čevlji
cloakroom	garderoba
clock	ura
close adj	zaprt(-a/-o)
close vb	zapreti
closed (sign)	zaprto
cloth (fabric)	blago
clothes	obleke
cloudy: it's cloudy	oblačno je
clove (spice)	klinček
club	klub
coach (bus)	avtobus
coach trip	izlet z avtobusom
coast	obala
coastguard	obalna straža
coat	plašč
coat hanger	obešalnik
cocoa	čokoladno mleko
coconut	kokosov oreh
code: dialling code	klicna številka
postcode	poštna številka
coffee	kava
black coffee	črna kava
white coffee	bela kava
decaffeinated coffee	kava brez kafeina
coin	kovanec
Coke®	koka-kola
colander	cedilo
cold n (illness)	prehlad
I have a cold	prehlajen(-a) sem
cold adj	mrzel(-zla/-o)

I'm cold	zebe me
it's cold	mrzlo je
cold water	hladna voda
collect	zbirati
colour	barva
colour film *(for camera)*	barvni film
comb	glavnik
come *(arrive)*	prispeti
come in!	naprej!
comfortable	udoben(-bna/-o)
company *(firm)*	podjetje ; firma
compartment *(in train)*	oddelek ; kupe
compass	kompas
competitor	konkurent(-ka)
complaint	reklamacija
complicated	kompliciran(-a/-o)
compulsory	obvezen(-zna/-o)
computer	računalnik
computer disk *(floppy)*	gibki disk
concert	koncert
concert hall	koncertna dvorana
condom	kondom
conductor *(on bus)*	sprevodnik
conference	konferenca
confirm	potrditi
confused	zmeden(-a/-o)
congratulations	čestitke
connection *(train, etc)*	veza ; zveza
consulate	konzulat
contact *vb*	obrniti se na
contact lens(es)	leča(e)
contact lens cleaner	čistilo za leče

contraceptive	kontracepcija
cook *vb*	kuhati
cooker	štedilnik
cool	hladen(-dna/-o)
cool-box	hladilna torba
copy *n (duplicate)*	prepis
corkscrew	odčepnik
corner	vogal
cost: how much does it cost?	koliko stane?
costume *(swimming)*	kopalna obleka
cotton	bombaž
cotton wool	vata
cough *vb*	kašljati
counter *(in shop, bar, etc)*	prodajna miza
country *(nation)*	država
courgettes	bučke
course *(of meal)*	obrok
main course	glavna jed
(of study)	tečaj
cow	krava
crab	rakovica
craftsman(woman)	rokodelec(-lka)
crampons	dereze
crash *n (car)*	trčenje
crash helmet	zaščitna čelada
cream *(lotion)*	krema
(on milk)	smetana
credit card	kreditna kartica
crisis	kriza
crisps	čips
cross *n*	križ
cross country skiing	tek na smučeh

crossroads	prečna cesta
crossword puzzle	križanka
crowd	množica
crowded	natrpan(-a/-o)
crown (on tooth)	krona
cruise n	križarjenje
cry vb (weep)	jokati
cucumber	kumara
cultivate	gojiti
cup	skodelica
cupboard	element ; kuhinjska omarica
currant	ribez
current n (electric)	tok
curtain	zavesa
cushion	blazina
custom (tradition)	navada
customer	stranka
cutoms (duty)	carina
cut n	rez
cut vb	rezati ; vrezati
cutlery	jedilni pribor
cycle (bicycle)	kolo
daily adj	dneven(-vna/-o)
damage n	škoda
damp	vlažen(-žna/-o)
dance n	ples
dance vb	plesati
dangerous	nevaren(-rna/-o)
dark	temen(-mna/-o)

after dark	ko se stemni
date	datum
date of birth	datum rojstva
daughter	hči
my daughter	moja hči
dawn	zarja
day	dan
1 day	en dan
2 days	dva dni
3 days	tri dni
per day	na dan
dead	mrtev(-tva)
deaf	gluh(-a/-o)
death	smrt
debt	dolg
decaffeinated coffee	kava brez kafeina
December	december
deckchair	ležalnik
deep	globok(-a/-o)
deer	srna
defrost	odtaliti
delay *n*	zamuda
delayed:the train is delayed	vlak ima zamudo
delicatessen	delikatese
delicious	slasten(-tna/-o)
dentist	zobozdravnik(-nica)
dentures	umetno zobovje
deodorant	deodorant
department	oddelek
department store	veleblagovnica
departures	odhodi
deposit *n*	naplačilo

desk	urad
dessert	slaščice
details	podrobnosti
detergent	pralno sredstvo
detour *n*	obvoz
develop *(photos)*	razviti
diabetic: I'm diabetic	sladkorni bolnik sem
dial *vb*	zavrteti številko
dialect	narečje
dialling code	klicna številka
diamond	diamant
diarrhoea	driska
diary	koledarček
dictionary	slovar
diesel	diesel
diet	dijeta
I'm on a diet	imam dijeto
different	drugačen(-čna/-o)
difficult	težek(-žka/-o)
dining room	jedilnica
dinner *(evening meal)*	večerja
when is dinner?	kdaj je večerja?
direct train	direktni vlak
directory *(telephone)*	telefonski imenik
directory enquiries	informacije
dirty	umazan(-a/-o)
disabled *(person)*	invalid
disappear	izginiti
disappointed	razočaran(-a/-o)
disaster	katastrofa
disco	disco
discount	popust

dish	jed
side dish	prikuha
dishwasher	pomivalni stroj
disinfectant	razkužilo
disk *(computer)*	disk
display *n*	razstava
display *vb*	razstaviti
distance	razdalja
distilled water	destilirana voda
divorced	ločen(-a)
DIY	napravi si sam
do	delati
doctor	zdravnik(-ca)
documents	dokumenti
dog	pes
doll	lutka
dollar	dolar
donkey	opica
door	vrata
double	dvojen
double bed	zakonska postelja
double room	dvoposteljna soba
down	spodaj ; dol
go down	iti dol
downstairs	spodaj
drain *n*	odvodni kanal
draught *(of air)*	prepih
draught lager	točeno pivo
drawer	predal
drawing	risanje
dress *n*	obleka
dress oneself *vb*	obleči se

dressing *(for food)*	začimbe
drill *(tool)*	sveder
drink *n*	pijača
drink *vb*	piti
drinking water	pitna voda
drive	voziti ; peljati
driver	voznik(-ca)
driving licence	vozniško dovoljenje
drought	suša
drown	utoniti
drunk	pijan(-a)
drug *(medicine)*	zdravilo
dry *adj*	suh(-a/-o)
dry *vb*	sušiti
dry-cleaner's	čistilnica
duck	raca
dummy *(for baby)*	cucelj
during	med
dust *n*	prah
duty-free shop	duty-free trgovina
duvet	odeja

ear	uho
ears	ušesa
earache	bolečine v ušesih
earlier	bolj zgodaj
early	zgodaj
ear-phones	slušalke
earrings	uhani
earth *(soil)*	zemlja

earthquake	potres
east	vzhod
Easter	velika noč
easy	lahek(-hka/-o)
eat	jesti
edge	rob
egg	jajce
eggs	jajca
fried egg	pečeno jajce
hard-boiled egg	trdo kuhano jajce
scrambled eggs	umešana jajca
elastic band	elastika
electric	električen(-čna/-o)
electrician	električar
electricity	elektrika
electric fire	električna sobna peč
electric shaver	električni brivnik
elegant	eleganten(-tna/-o)
elevator	dvigalo
embassy	veleposlalništvo
emergency	nuja
emergency exit	zasilni izhod
employment	zaposlitev
empty	prazen(-zna/-o)
end	konec
engaged *(to be married)*	zaročen(-a)
(phone, toilet, etc)	zaseden(-a/-o)
engine	stroj ; motor
engineer	inženir
England	Anglija
English	Anglež(-inja)
enjoy: I enjoy swimming	rad(-a) plavam

I enjoy dancing	rad(-a) plešem
enormous	ogromen(-mna/-o)
enough: that's enough	to je dovolj
enquiry desk	informacijski urad
enter	vstopiti
entertainment	razvedrilo
entrance	vstop
entrance fee	vstopnina
envelope	kuverta
equipment	oprema
escalator	eskalator
escape *vb*	pobegniti
especially	posebno
Eurocheque	Euroček
Europe	Evropa
European Union	Evropska Unija
eve	večer
Christmas Eve	božični večer
New Year's Eve	novoletni večer
evening	večer
this evening	danes zvečer
tomorrow evening	jutri zvečer
in the evening	zvečer
evening meal	večerja
every	vsak
everyone	vsakdo
everything	vse
examination *(medical)*	pregled
example: for example	na primer
excellent	odličen(-čna/-o)
except	razen
exchange *vb*	zamenjati

exchange rate	menjalni tečaj
exciting	razburljiv(-a/-o)
excursion	ekskurzija
excuse: excuse me!	oprostite!
exhaust pipe	izpušna cev
exhibition	razstava
exit	izhod
emergency exit	zasilni izhod
fire exit	izhod v primeru požara
expense	izdatek
expensive	drag(-a/-o)
expire *(ticket, etc)*	poteči ; končati se
explain	razložiti
extra	dodaten(-na/-o)
an extra bed	dodatna postelja
an extra towel	dodatna brisača
eye	oko
eyes	oči

fabric	tkanina
face	obraz
(of mountain)	stena
facilities	možnosti ; pripomočki
factory	tovarna
faint *vb*	omedleti
fair *(hair)*	svetlolas(-a)
fall	pasti
he has fallen	padel je
she has fallen	padla je
family	družina

my family	moja družina
famous	slaven(-vna/-o)
fan (hand-held)	pahljača
(electric)	ventilator
far	daleč
is it far?	je daleč?
fare (train, bus, etc)	vozovnica
farm	kmetija
farmer	kmet(-ica)
farm holiday	kmečki turizem
farming	kmetijstvo
fashion	moda
fast adv	hitro
fat	debel(-a/-o)
father	oče ; ata
my father	moj oče ; moj ata
father-in-law	tast
fault (defect)	napaka
favourite	najljubši(-a/-o)
fax	fax ; faks
by fax	po faxu
feather	pero
February	februar
feed vb	hraniti
feel: I feel sick	slabo mi je
feet	noge
fellow	fant ; možak
ferry	trajekt
festival	festival
fetch	iti po ; prinesti
fever	vročina
few	malo ; nekaj

fiancé	zaročenec
my fiancé	moj zaročenec
fiancée	zaročenka
my fiancée	moja zaročenka
figs	smokve
fight n	boj ; bitka
file (for papers)	register za dokumente
filing cabinet	kartoteka
filigree	filigran
fill up	napolniti
fill it up!	napolni!
filling (in tooth)	plomba
film	film
filter	filter
find	najti
fine n	kazen
finger	prst
fingers	prsti
finish	končati
fire	požar
fire alarm	požarni alarm
fire brigade	gasilci
fire escape	izhod v primeru požara
fire extinguisher	naprava za gašenje ognja
fireworks	ognjemet
first	prvi(-a/-o)
first aid kit	komplet za prvo pomoč
first class	prvi razred
first floor	prvo nadstropje
fish n	ribe
fish vb	ribariti ; loviti ribe
fisherman	ribič

fishing net	ribiška mreža
fishing permit	dovoljenje za ribolov
fishing rod	ribiška palica
fishmonger's	ribarnica
fit vb : it doesn't fit me	ne pristoja mi
fix vb	popraviti
flag	zastava
flash	blisk
flat n (apartment)	stanovanje
flat adj	raven(-vna/-o)
flat tyre	prazna guma
flaw	napaka
flavour	okus
fleas	bolhe
flight	polet
flippers	plavuti
flood n	poplava
floor	nadstropje
which floor?	v katerem nadstropju
ground floor	pritličje
florist's shop	cvetličarna
flour	moka
flowers	cvetlice ; rože
flu	gripa
fly n	muha
fly vb	leteti
fog	megla
foggy: it's foggy	megleno je
foil (silver paper)	staniol
follow	slediti
food	hrana
food poisoning	zastrupitev z hrano

foot *(body)*	noga
feet	noge
football	nogomet
for	za
for me	zame
for him/her	zanj/za njo
for us	za nas
foreign	tuj(-a/-e)
forecast	napoved
weather forecast	vremenska napoved
forest	gozd
forever	za vedno
forget	pozabiti
fork *(for eating)*	vilica
form *(document)*	formular
fortnight	štirinajst dni
fortress	trdnjava
forwards	naprej
fountain	studenec ; vodnjak
fox	lisica
fracture *n*	zlom
fragrant	dišeč(-a/-e)
France	Francija
free *(unoccupied)*	prosto
free of charge	brezplačen(-čna/-o)
freezer	zmrzovalnik
French	Francoz(-inja)
French fries	pommes frites
frequently	pogosto
fresh	svež(-a/-e)
Friday	petek
fridge	hladilnik

fried	ocvrt(-a/-o)
friend	prijatelj(-ica)
frog	žaba
from	iz ; od
from Scotland	iz Škotske
from England	iz Anglije
from faraway	od daleč
front: in front of…	pred
frozen	zmrznjen(-a/-o)
fruit	sadje
stewed fruit	kompot
fruit juice	sadni sok
fruit salad	sadna solata
frying pan	ponev
full	poln(-a/-o)
(occupied)	zasedeno
full board	polni penzion
fumes *(of car)*	dim
funeral	pogreb
funfair	lunapark
funny	smešen(-šna/-o)
fur coat	krzneni plašč
furniture	pohištvo
fuse	varovalka

gallery	galerija
gallon	= approx. 4.5 litres
game	igra
(meat)	divjačina

garage (private)	garaža
(for repairs)	avtomehanik
garden	vrt
garlic	česen
gas	plin
gas cylinder	plinska bomba
gas cooker	plinski kuhalnik
gate (airport)	izhod
gear	prestava
reverse gear	vzvratna prestava
generous	radodaren(-rna/-o)
gentleman	gospod
Gents' (toilet)	MOŠKI
German (person)	Nemec(-mka)
German measles	rdečke
Germany	Nemčija
get (obtain)	dobiti
get in	vstopiti
get off	izstopiti
gift	darilo
gift shop	spominki
gin and tonic	gin s tonikom
ginger (spice)	ingver
girl	dekle
girlfriend	punca
my girlfriend	moja punca
give	dati
give back	dati nazaj
glacier	ledenik
glass (to drink out of)	kozarec
a glass of water	kozarec vode
a glass of wine	kozarec vina

glasses (specatacles)	očala
gloves	rokavice
glue	lepilo
go	iti
I'm going to...	grem v...
we're going to...	gremo v...
go back	iti nazaj
go down	iti dol
go in	iti noter
go out	iti ven
God	bog
godfather	boter
godmother	botra
gold (metal)	zlato
golf	golf
golf clubs	oprema za golf
golf course	igrišče za golf
good	dober(-bra/-o)
goodbye	na svidenje
good day	dober dan
good evening (from 6pm)	dober večer
good morning	dobro jutro
good night	lahko noč
goose	gos
gramme	gram
grandfather	stari oče
grandmother	stara mama
grapefruit	grenivka
grapes	grozdje
grass	trava
greasy	masten(-tna/-o)
great (big)	velik(-a/-o)

Great Britain	Velika Britanija
green	zelen(-a/-o)
green card (car insurance)	zelena karta
grey	siv(-a/-o)
grilled	na žaru
grocer's	špecerija
ground floor	pritličje
on the ground floor	v pritličju
group	skupina
grow vb	rasti
(cultivate)	gojiti
guarantee n	jamstvo
guard	stražar
guest	gost(-a)
guesthouse	penzion
guide	vodič
guidebook	vodič
guided tour	ogled z vodičem
guitar	kitara
gym shoes	telovadni copati

haemorrhoids	hemeroidi
hail n	toča
hair	lasje
hairbrush	krtača za lase
haircut	striženje las
hairdresser	frizer (-ka)
hair dryer	fen ; sušilec ža lase
hair dye	barva za lase

lf	polovica ; pol
a half bottle of...	pol steklenice...
half an hour	pol ure
half board	pol penzion
half-price	polovična cena
ham	šunka
hammer	kladivo
hand	roka
handbag	torbica
handicapped (person)	invalid
handkerchief	robec
hand luggage	ročna prtljaga
hand-made	ročno izdelano
hanger (coathanger)	obešalnik
happen	zgoditi se
what happened?	kaj se je zgodilo?
happy	vesel(-a/-o) ; srečen(-čna/-o)
happy birthday!	vse najboljše za rojstni dan
harbour	pristanišče
hard	težek(-žka/-o)
harvest n	žetev
hat	klobuk
have	imeti
I have...	imam...
I don't have...	nimam...
we have...	imamo...
we don't have...	nimamo...
do you have...?	ali imate...?
hay fever	seneni nahod
hazelnuts	lešniki
he	on ; see GRAMMAR
head	glava

headache	glavobol
I have a headache	glava me boli
headlights	prednja luči na avtu
health resort	zdravilišče
hear	slišati
hearing aid	slušalka
heart	srce
heart attack	srčni napad
heater	grelec
heavy	težek(-žka/-o)
height	višina
hello	pozdravljeni
help n	pomoč
help!	na pomoč!
help vb	pomagati
can you help me?	mi lahko pomagate?
hepatitis	hepatitis
her...	njen(-a/-o)
her passport	njen potni list
her room	njena soba
her bike	njeno kolo
herb	zelišče
here	tukaj
here is...	izvolite...
here is my passport	izvolite moj potni list
high	visok(-a/-o)
high tide	plima
high blood pressure	visok krvni pritisk
highchair	otroški stolček
hill	hrib
hill-walking	hoja v hribih
hip	bok

hire n	najem
car hire	najeti avto
bike hire	najeti kolo
boat hire	najeti čoln
ski hire	najeti smuči
hire vb	najeti
his...	njegov(-a/-o)
his passport	njegov potni list
his room	njegova soba
his bike	njegovo kolo
hitchhike	potovati z avtoštopom
hold (contain)	vsebovati
hold-up (traffic)	zastoj v prometu
hole	luknja
holiday	dopust
on holiday	na dopustu
home	dom
at home	doma
homesick	domotožje
I'm homesick	domotožje imam
honey	med
honeymoon	medeni tedni
hope: I hope so	upam, da
I hope not	upam, da ne
horse	konj
horse riding	jahanje
hospital	bolnišnica
hospital ward	oddelek v bolnišnici
hostel	dom ; koča
hot	vroč(-a/-e)
I'm hot	vroče mi je
it's hot	vroče je

hot chocolate	kakav
hot water	topla voda
hotel	hotel
hour	ura
2 hours	dve uri
half an hour	pol ure
house	hiša
how	kako
how much/many?	koliko?
how are you?	kako vam gre?
hungry: I'm hungry	lačen(-čna) sem
hunting permit	dovoljenje za lov
hurry: I'm in a hurry	mudi se mi
hurt	boleti
that hurts	to boli
husband	mož
my husband	moj mož
hut (mountain)	koča
hydrofoil	gliser

I	jaz ; see GRAMMAR
ice	led
ice tea	ledeni čaj
ice coffee	ledena kava
with ice	z ledom
ice-axe	cepin
ice cream	sladoled
ice rink	drsališče
ice skates	drsalke
identity card	osebna izkaznica

if	če
ignition	vžig
ill	bolan(-lna/-o)
I'm ill	bolan(bolna) sem
immediately	takoj
impatient	nepotrpežljiv(-a/-o)
important	pomemben(-bna/-o)
impossible: it's impossible	nemogoče je
in	v ; na
in 2 hours	čez dva uri
in London	v Londonu
inch	= approx. 2.5cm
included	vlkjučen(-čna/-o)
indicator *(in car)*	smerno kazalo
indigestion	slaba prebava
infectious	nalezljiv(-a/-o)
information	informacije
information office	informacije
ingredients	sestavine
injection	injekcija
injured	poškodovan(-a/-o)
ink	črnilo
inn	gostilna
insect	mrčes
insect repellent	prašek
inside	notri
instant coffee	instant kava
instead	namesto
instructor	inštruktor(-ica)
insulin	insulin
insurance	zavarovanje
interesting	zanimiv(-a/-o)

international	mednarodni(-a/-o)
interpreter	tolmač
interval	odmor
interview n	intervju
into	v
into town	v mesto
into the centre	v središče mesta
invitation	povabilo
invite	povabiti
invoice	račun ; faktura
Ireland	Irska
Irish	Irec (Irka)
iron (metal)	železo
(for clothes)	likalnik
iron vb	likati
is	see GRAMMAR
island	otok
it	see GRAMMAR
Italian	Italijan(-ka)
Italy	Italija
itch vb	srbeti

jack (for car)	dvigalo za avtomobile
jacket	jopič ; suknjič
jam	marmelada
jammed (stuck)	blokiran(-a/-o)
January	januar
jar	vrč
jaundice	zlatenica
jeans	jeans

jelly	žele
jellyfish	meduza
jeweller's	zlatarna
jewellery	nakit
job	delo
jog: to go jogging	teči
joke *n*	šala
journalist	novinar(-ka)
journey	potovanje
jug	vrč
juice	sok
apple juice	jabolčni sok
orange juice	pomaranči sok
tomato juice	paradižnikov sok
July	julij
jump *n*	skok
jump *vb*	skakati
junction *(traffic)*	križišče
June	junij

keep	obdržati
key	ključ
my key	moj kluč
keyring	obesek za ključe
kidneys	ledvice
kilo	kilogram
a kilo of apples	en kilogram jabolk
2 kilos	dva kilograma
kilometre	kilometer
10 kilometres	deset kilometrov

king	kralj
kind *adj*	ljubezniv(-a/-o)
kiosk	kiosk
kiss *n*	poljub
kiss *vb*	poljubiti
kitchen	kuhinja
kitten	mucek
knee	koleno
knickers	spodnje hlače
knife	nož
knot	vozel
know: I don't know	ne vem
label	etiketa
lace	čipka
laces *(for shoes)*	vezalke
ladder	lestev
Ladies' *(toilet)*	ŽENSKE
lager	pivo
draught lager	točeno pivo
lake	jezero
Lake Bled	Blejsko jezero
lamb	jagnje
lamp	svetilka
landing *(of plane)*	pristanek
landlady	hišna lastnica
landlord	hišni lastnik
language	jezik
large	velik(-a/-o)
last	zadnji(-a/-e)

the last bus	zadnji avtobus
the last train	zadnji vlak
last night	včeraj zvečer
last week	prejšnji teden
last year	lani
late	pozno
sorry we are late	oprostite, pozni smo
later	kasneje
launderette	pralnica
lavatory	stranišče
lawyer	pravnik(-ca) ; odvetnik(-ca)
leader	vodja
leaf	list
leak *n*	luknja
there is a leak	to je preluknjano
leak *vb*	puščati ; curljati
learn	učiti se ; naučiti se
lease *(rental)*	najemnina
leather	usnje
leave	oditi ; odpeljati
when does the bus leave?	kdaj odpelje avtobus?
when does the train leave?	kdaj odpelje vlak?
leeks	por
left	levo
on/to the left	na levo
left-luggage *(office)*	garderoba
leg	noga
lemon	limona
lemonade	limonada
lemon tea	čaj z limono
lend	posoditi
length	dolžina

lens (contact lens)	optična leča
lentils	leča
less	manj
lesson	lekcija
let (allow)	dovoliti
(lease)	dati v najem
letter	pismo
(of alphabet)	črka
letterbox	poštni nabiralnik
lettuce	zelena solata
library	knjižnica
licence (driving)	vozniško dovoljenje
lid	pokrov
lie down	uleči se
life	življenje
lifeboat	rešilni pas
lifeguard	telesna straža
life insurance	življensko zavarovanje
lift (elevator)	dvigalo
can you give me a lift?	me lahko zapeljete?
light n	luč
have you got a light?	imate vžigalnik?
light adj (not heavy)	lahek(-hka/-o)
lightbulb	žarnica
lighter	vžigalnik
lightning	bliskanje
like prep	kakor ; kot
it's like this	tako je
like vb	rad(-a) imeti
I like coffee	rad(-a) imam kavo
I'd like...	želim...
we'd like...	želimo...

lime *(tree)*	lipa
line	linija
lingerie	fino damsko perilo
lips	ustnice
lipstick	rdečilo za ustnice
liqueurs	likerji
list	seznam
listen (to)	poslušati
litre	liter
a litre of milk	en liter mleka
litter *(rubbish)*	odpadki
little: a little	malo
live	živeti ; stanovati
he lives in London	on živi v Londonu
I live in a flat	stanujem v stanovanju
liver	jetra
living room	dnevna soba
lizard	kuščar
loaf	hlebec
a loaf of bread	hlebec kruha
lobster	jastog
lock *vb*	zakleniti
lock *n*	ključavnica
locker *(for luggage)*	omarica
London	London
in London	v Londonu
to London	v London
long	dolg(-a/-o)
for a long time	za dolgo časa
look	gledati ; pogledati
look after	paziti
look for	iskati

lorry	kamion
lose *vb*	izgubiti
I 've lost my wallet	izgubil(-a) sem denarnico
lost	izgubljen(-a/-o)
I 'm lost	izgubljen(-a) sem
lost property office	urad za izgubljene predmete
lot: a lot	veliko
loud *(noisy)*	hrupen(-pna/-o)
lounge	dnevna soba
(in airport)	čakalnica
love *n*	ljubezen
love *vb*	ljubiti
I love you	ljubim te
lovely	ljubek(-bka/-o)
low	nizek(-zka/-o)
low tide	oseka
lucky	srečen(-čna/-o)
luggage	prtljaga
hand luggage	ročna prtljaga
luggage rack	polica za prtljago
luggage tag	naslovna tablica
luggage trolley	voziček za prtljago
lunch	kosilo
luxury	luksuz ; izobilje
machine	stroj
magazine	revija
maid	služkinja
maiden name	dekliško ime
main	glavni(-vna/-o)

main course *(of meal)*	glavna jed
mains *(electrical, water)*	glavni vod napeljave
make	narediti ; napraviti
make-up	kozmetika
man	mož
men	moški
manager	direktor(-ica)
many	mnogo
map	zemljevid ; karta ; plan
road map	cestna karta
detailed map *(one-inch)*	specialka
marble	marmor
March	marec
margarine	margarina
market	tržnica
where is the market?	kje je tržnica?
when is the market?	kdaj je odprta tržnica?
marmalade	pomarančna marmelada
married	poročen(-a)
I'm married	poročen(-a) sem
are you married?	ste poročeni?
mass *(church)*	masa
match *(game)*	tekma
matches	vžigalice
material	material
matter: it doesn't matter	nič za to
May	maj
meadow	travnik
meal	jed
mean *vb*	pomeniti
what does this mean?	kaj to pomeni?
measles	ošpice

meat	meso
white meat	belo meso
red meat	rdeče meso
mechanic	mehanik
medicine	medicina
medium rare *(meat)*	malo pečen(-a/-o)
meet	srečati
meeting	srečanje
melon	melona
watermelon	lubenica
melt	topiti
member	član
men	ljudje
menu	jedilni list
meringue	beljakova pena
message	sporočilo
meter	števec
metre	meter
microwave oven	mikrovalovna pečica
midday	opoldan
at midday	opoldne
midnight	polnoč
at midnight	ob polnoči
migraine	migrena
I have a migraine	migreno imam
mile	5 miles = 8km
milk	mleko
fresh milk	sveže mleko
long-life milk	dolgotrajno mleko
powdered milk	mleko v prahu
skimmed milk	posneto mleko
millimetre	milimeter

million	milijon
2 million	dva milijona
mince *(meat)*	mleto meso
mind: I don't mind	vseeno mi je
mineral water	mineralna voda
minor road	stranska cesta
minute	minuta
10 minutes	deset minut
mirror	ogledalo
miss *(plane, train, etc)*	zamuditi
Miss	gospodična
missing *(thing)*	manjkajoč(-a/-e)
(person)	pogrešan(-a/-o)
mistake	napaka
misunderstanding	nesporazum
modern	modern(-a/-o)
moisture	vlaga
moisture-proof	odporen(-rna/-o) proti vlagi
moment: at the moment	trenutno
monastery	samostan
Monday	ponedeljek
money	denar
I have no money	nimam nič denarja
month	mesec
1 month	en mesec
3 months	tri mesece
this month	ta mesec
last month	prejšnji mesec
next month	naslednji mesec
monument	spomenik
moon	luna
more	več ; še

more than 3	več kot tri
more bread, please	še kruha, prosim
more water, please	še vode, prosim
morning	jutro
in the morning	zjutraj
this morning	danes zjutraj
tomorow morning	jutri zutraj
mosquito	komar
moths (clothes)	molji
mother	mama ; mati
my mother	moja mama ; moja mati
mother-in-law	tašča
motor	motor
motorboat	motorni čoln
motorcycle	motorno kolo
motorway	avtocesta
mountain	gora
mountain bike	gorsko kolo
mountain hut	planinska koča
mountain pass	sedlo
mountaineering	alpinizem
mouse	miš
moustache	brki
mouth	usta
Mr	gospod
Mrs	gospa
Ms	gospa
much	veliko
too much	preveč
muscle	mišica
museum	muzej
mushrooms	gobe

music	glasba
mussels	školjke
must	morati
mustard	gorčica
mutton	bravina
my...	moj(-a/-o)
my passport	moj potni list
my room	moja soba
my bike	moje kolo
nail *(metal)*	žebelj
(on finger)	noht
nail polish	lak za nohte
nail polish remover	odstranjevalec laka za nohte
naked	gol(-a/-o)
name	ime
my name is...	ime mi je...
what is your name? *(familiar)*	kako ti je ime?
what is your name? *(polite)*	kako vam je ime?
napkin	servieta
nappy	plenica
narrow	ozek(-zka/-o)
national	naroden(-na/-o)
nationality	državljanstvo
navy blue	temno moder(-dra/-o)
near	blizu
is it near?	je blizu?
necessary	potreben(-bna/-o)
neck	vrat
necklace	ogrlica

need: I need…	potrebujem…
we need…	potrebujemo…
needle	šivanka
a needle and thread	šivanka in sukanec
negative (photography)	negativ
neighbour	sosed(-a)
nephew	nečak
my nephew	moj nečak
never	nikoli
I never drink wine	nikoli ne pijem vina
new	nov(-a/-o)
news (on television)	poročila
newspaper	časopis
newsstand	kiosk
New Year	novo leto
happy New Year!	srečno novo leto!
New Zealand	Nova Zelandija
next	naslednji(-a/-e)
next week	naslednji teden
the next bus	naslednji avtobus
the next train	naslednji vlak
nice	lep(-a/-o) ; prijeten(-tna/-o)
niece	nečakinja
my niece	moja nečakinja
night	noč
at night	ponoči
per night	na noč
tomorrow night (evening)	jutri zvečer
nightclub	nočni klub
nightdress	spalna srajca
no	ne
no thanks	ne hvala

(without)	brez
no sugar	brez sladkorja
no ice	brez leda
nobody	nihče
noisy	hrupen(-pna/-o)
it's very noisy	zelo hrupno je
non-alcoholic	brezalkoholen(-lna/-o)
none: there's none left	nič ni ostalo
non-smoking	nekadilci
north	sever
Northern Ireland	Severna Irska
nose	nos
not	ne
I don't know	ne vem
note *(written)*	zapisek
note pad	beležnica
nothing	nič
November	november
now	sedaj
number	številka
number plate *(car)*	avtomobilska registerska tablica
nurse	medicinska sestra
nuts	orehi
oars	vesla
occasionally	tu in tam ; občasno
October	oktober
octopus	hobotnica
of	iz ; od
a bottle of wine	steklenica vina

a glass of water	kozarec vode
north of...	severno od...
made of...	narejeno iz...
off *(radio, engine, etc) adj*	ugasnjen(-a/-o)
(milk, food)	pokvarjen(-a/-o)
office	pisarna
often	pogosto
how often?	kako pogosto?
oil	olje
ointment	mazilo
OK	prav ; OK
old	star(-a/-o)
how old are you?	koliko ste stari?
olive oil	olivno olje
olives	olive
omelette	omleta
on *(radio, engine, etc) adj*	prižgan(-a/-o)
on *adv*	na
on the table	na mizi
on time	točen(-čna/-o)
once	enkrat
one	eden ; en
one-way road	enosmerna cesta
onion	čebula
only	samo
open *(sign)*	odprto
open *vb*	odpreti
opera	opera
operator *(telephone)*	telefonist(-ka)
opposite	nasproti
opposite the hotel	nasproti hotela
opposite the bank	nasproti banke

optician	optik
or	ali
tea or coffee	kavo ali čaj
orange *adj*	oranžen(-žna/-o)
orange *n*	pomaranča
orange juice	pomarančni sok
orchard	sadovnjak
orchestra	orkester
order *vb*	naročiti
order: out of order	pokvarjeno
organize	organizirati
other	drug(-a/-o)
ounce	= approx. 30g
our	naš(-a/-e)
our car	naš avto
our room	naša soba
our town	naše mesto
ours	naši
out	ven
he's gone out	ven je šel
outside	zunaj
outskirts	periferija
oven	pečica
overcharge *vb*	preveč zaračunati
overtake *(in car)*	prehitevati
owe	dolgovati
you owe me...	dolgujete mi...
owner	lastnik(-ca)
oyster	ostriga

pack vb (bags)	pakirati
packet	paket
padlock	mala ključavnica
paid: I've paid	plačal(-a) sem
pain	bolečina
painful	boleč(-a/-e)
painkiller	zdravilo proti bolečinam
paint (picture) vb	slikati
painting n	slika
pair	par
palace	palača
pan	ponev
pancake	palačinka
pants (underwear)	spodnje hlače
paper	papir
parcel	paket
pardon: I beg your pardon	oprostite!
parents	starši
my parents	moji starši
park n	park
park vb	parkirati
parking disk	parkirna ura
parking meter	parkirna ura
parsley	peteršilj
partner (business)	partner
(friend)	soprog(-a)
party (celebration)	zabava
(political)	stranka
pass (mountain)	sedlo
passenger	potnik(-ica)
passport	potni list
my passport	moj potni list

pasta	testenine
pastry	pecivo
paté	pašteta
path	pot ; steza
pavement	pločnik
pay *vb*	plačati
I want to pay	želim plačati
payment	plačilo
peace	mir
peach	breskve
4 peaches	štiri breskve
peak rate	najvišja cena
peanuts	lešniki (kiki-riki)
pearls	biseri
pears	hruške
4 pears	štiri hruške
peas	grah
pedestrian	pešec
pedestrian crossing	prehod za pešce
peel *vb (fruit)*	olupiti
peg *(for rock climbing)*	klin
pen	pero
pencil	svinčnik
penicillin	penicilin
penknife	žepni nož
pensioner	upokojenec(-ka)
pepper	poper
(vegetable)	paprika
per	na
per day	na dan
per hour	na uro
per week	na teden

perfect	odličen(-čna/-o)
performance	predstava
perfume	parfum
period *(menstruation)*	menstruacija
perm	trajna
permit *n*	dovoljenje
fishing permit	dovoljenje za ribolov
hunting permit	dovoljenje za lov
person: per person	na osebo
petrol	bencin
4-star petrol	super
unleaded petrol	neosvinčeni bencin
petrol station	bencinska črpalka
pewter	kositer
phone *n*	telefon
by phone	po telefonu
phone *vb*	telefonirati
phonebox	telefonska kabina
phonecard	telefonska kartica
photocopy *n*	fotokopija
I need a photocopy	poptrebujem fotokopijo
photocopy *vb*	fotokopirati
photograph	fotografija
piano	klavir
picnic	piknik
picture *(on wall)*	slika
pie	pito
apple pie	jabolčno pito
piece	kos
a piece of that, please	kos tega, prosim
pier	pomol
pill	pilula ; tableta

the Pill *(contraceptive)*	kontraceptcijske tablete
pillow	blazina
pillowcase	prevleka za blazino
pin	bucika
pineapple	ananas
pine tree	bor
pink	roza
pint	= approx. 0.5litre
pipe *(for smoking)*	pipa
(drain,etc)	cev
pizzeria	picerija
place	prostor
plane	letalo
plaster *(sticking)*	obliž
plastic	plastičen(-čna/-o)
plastic bag	plastična vrečka
plate	krožnik
platform *(railway)*	peron
which platform?	kateri peron
play n	igra
play vb	igrati
playroom	igralnica
please	prosim
pleased: pleased to meet you	me veseli
pliers	klešče
plug *(electric)*	vtikač
(for sink)	zamašek
plum brandy	slivovka
plums	slive
plumber	inštalater
poison	strup
poisonous	strupen(-a/-o)

police *(force)*	policija
police officer	policist(-ka)
police station	policijska postaja
polish *(for shoes)*	krema za čevlje
polluted	onesnažen(-a/-o)
poor	reven(-vna/-o)
popular	priljubljen(-a/-o)
pork	svinjina
port *(harbour)*	pristanišče
(drink)	port
porter *(for door)*	vratar
(for luggage)	postrešček
post: by post	po pošti
post *vb*	poslati
postbox	poštni nabiralnik
postcard	razglednica
postcode	poštna številka
poster	plakat
post office	pošta
pot *(for cooking)*	lonec
potato	krompir
boiled potatoes	kuhan krompir
sautéed potatoes	pražen krompir
mashed potatoes	pire krompir
potato salad	krompirjeva solata
pottery	lončarstvo
pound *(money)*	funt
(weight)	= approx. 0.5 kilo
powdered milk	mleko v prahu
prayer	molitev
prefer	rajši imeti
pregnant: I'm pregnant	noseča sem

prepare	pripraviti
prescription	recept
present *(gift)*	darilo
pressure: tyre pressure	pritisk v zračnicah
pretty	ljubek(-bka/-o)
price	cena
price list	cenik
priest	duhovnik
prince	princ
princess	princesa
print *(photo)*	kopija
private	zaseben(-bna/-o)
prize	nagrada
probably	verjetno
problem	problem
programme *(TV, radio)*	spored
prohibited	prepovedan(-a/-o)
pronounce *vb*	izgovoriti
how's this pronounced?	kako se to izgovori
prunes	suhe slive
public	javen(-vna/-o)
public holiday	praznik
publisher	založnik
pudding	sladica
pull *(sign on door)*	potegni
pullover	pulover
pump *(for bicycle)*	tlačilka za kolo
(petrol)	črpalka
puncture	luknjica
puppet show	lutkovna igra
purple	škrlaten(-a/-o)
purse	denarnica

push *(sign on door)*	rini
pushchair	otroški voziček
pyjamas	pižama

quality	kvaliteta
quay	pristan
queen	kraljica
question *n*	vprašanje
queue *n*	vrsta
queue *vb*	čakati v vrsti
quick	hiter(-tra/-o)
quickly	hitro
quiet *(place)*	miren(-rna/-o)
a quiet room	mirna soba
quilt	prešita odeja
quite: it's quite good	kar dobro je
it's quite expensive	precej drago je

rabbit	zajec
rabies	steklina
racket *(tennis, etc)*	lopar
radio	radio
radish	redkev
raffle	žrebanje
railway station	železniška postaja
rain *n*	dež
rainbow	mavrica
raincoat	dežni plašč

raining: it's raining	dežuje
raisins	rozine
rare	redek(-dka/-o)
(steak)	zelo malo pečen(-a/-o)
rash (skin)	izpuščaj
raspberries	maline
raspberry syrup	malinovec
rate of exchange	menjalni tečaj
raw	surov(-a/-o)
razor	brivski aparat
razor blades	britvice
read	brati
ready	pripravljen(-a/-o)
receipt	račun
recently	zadnje čase
reception (desk)	recepcija
recipe	recept
recommend	priporočati
record (disk)	gramofonska plošča
recover (from illness)	ozdraveti
red	rdeč(-a/-e)
redcurrant	rdeči ribez
reduction	znižanje
refill n	polnilo
refund n	povračilo
registered	prijavljen(-a/-o)
registration form	prijavnica
reimburse	povrniti stroške
relations (relatives)	sorodniki
relax	sprostiti se
remember	spomniti se
I don't remember	ne spomnim se

remind	spomniti
remind me	spomnite me
rent *n*	najemnina
rent *vb*	imeti v najemu
repair *vb*	popraviti
repeat *vb*	ponoviti
report *n*	poročilo
reservation	rezervacija
reserve	rezervirati
rest *n (relaxation)*	počitek
the rest of the wine	preostanek vina
rest *vb*	počivati
restaurant	restavracija
restaurant car	jedilni vagon
retired: I'm retired	upokojen(-a) sem
return *vb*	vrniti
return ticket	povratna vozovnica
reverse gear	vzvratna prestava
rheumatism	revma
rice	riž
rich *(person)*	bogat(-a/-o)
(food)	težka hrana
ride *(horse)*	jahati
ridge *(mountain)*	greben
riding school	jahalna šola
right *adj*	pravilen(-lna/-o)
right	desno
on/to the right	na desno
ring *(for fingers)*	prstan
ripe	zrel(-a/-o)
risotto	rižota
river	reka

road	cesta
road map	cestna karta
roast	pečenka
rock	skala
roll *(bread)*	žemlja
rollerblades	rolka
roller skate *(vb)*	kotalkati se
roller skates	kotalke
roof	streha
room *(of house, etc)*	soba
room number	številka sobe
my room number	številka moje sobe
room service	postrežba v sobi
rope	vrv
rose	vrtnica
rosé wine	roze vino
rotten *(fruit, etc)*	gnil(-a/-o)
round	okrogel(-gla-o)
route	smer
rowing *(sport)*	veslanje
rowing boat	čoln na vesla
royal	kraljevski(-ska-o)
rubber	guma
rubbish	odpadki
rucksack	nahrbtnik
rug *(for bed)*	debela odeja
(for floor)	majhna preproga
rush hour	ura najgostejšega prometa
rusty	rjast(-a/-o)

sad	žalosten(-tna-o)
safe *n*	trezor
safe: is it safe?	je varno?
safety pin	varnostna zaponka
sailing	jadranje
sailing boat	jadrnica
salad	solata
green salad	zelena solata
mixed salad	mešena solata
tomato salad	paradižikova solata
salad dressing	začimbe za solato
salami	salama
sales	razprodaja
salesperson	prodajalec(-lka)
salmon	losos
Danube salmon	sulec
salt	sol
sand	pesek
sandals	sandali
sandwich	sendvič
sanitary towel	higienski vložki
sardines	sardine
Saturday	sobota
sauce	omaka
saucepan	ponev
sauerkraut	kislo zelje
sauna	savna
sausage	klobasa
savoury	sočen(-čna-o)
say	reči
scarf	ruta
(wool/shawl)	šal

school	šola
scissors	škarje
score *(of match)*	rezultat
Scotland	Škotska
Scotsman(woman)	Škot(-inja)
screw *n*	vijak
screwdriver	izvijač
sculpture	kip
sea	morje
seafood	morski sadeži
seasickness	morska bolezen
seaside	obala
seat	sedež
seatbelt	varnostni pas
second *adj*	drugi(-a/-o)
second *n (time)*	sekunda
second class	drugi razred
second-hand goods	starine
secretary	tajnik(-ica)
see	videti
self-service	samopostrežna
sell	prodati ; prodajati
Sellotape®	lepilni trak
send	poslati
senior citizen	starejši občan
separate	ločen(-a)
September	september
serious	resen(-sna-o)
serve	streči
service: is service included?	je postrežba vključena?
serviette	servieta
sew	šivati

shade: in the shade	v senci
shallow	plitev(-tva-o)
shampoo	šampon
share *vb*	deliti
shave *vb*	briti
shaving cream	krema za britje
she	ona ; see GRAMMAR
sheep	ovca
sheet *(for bed)*	rjuha
shelf	polica
shellfish	školjke
ship	ladja
shirt	srajca
shock	pretres
shock absorber	amortizer
shoe	čevelj
my shoes	moji čevlji
shop	trgovina
shop assistant	trgovec(-vka)
shop window	izložba
shopping: to go shopping	iti nakupovat
shorts	kratke hlače
show *n*	predstava
show *vb*	pokazati
shower *(bath)*	prha ; tuš
(rain)	nevihta
shrimp	morski rakec
shut *(sign)*	zaprto
shut *vb*	zapreti
shutters	rolo
sick	bolan(-a/-o)
I feel sick	slabo mi je

sightseeing	ogled znamenitosti
side dish	prikuha
sign (notice)	znak
signature	podpis
silk	svila
silver (metal)	srebro
similar	podoben(-bna/-o)
simple	preprost(-a/-o)
sing	peti
single (not married)	samski(-ska)
single bed	postelja za eno osebo
single room	enoposteljna soba
sink n (washbasin)	umivalnik
sir	gospod
sister	sestra
my sister	moja sestra
sit	sedeti
size (of clothes, shoes)	številka
skate (on ice) vb	drsati se
skates (ice)	drsalke
(roller)	kotalke
skating	drsanje
ski vb	smučati
ski boots	smučarski čevlji
ski instructor	smučarski inštruktor
ski jump	smučarski skoki
ski lift	smučarska karta
ski pass	smučarska žičnica
ski run	tek na smučeh
skis	smuči
skimmed milk	posneto mleko
skin	koža

skirt	krilo
sky	nebo
sleep	spati
sleeper *(on train)*	spalnik
sleeping bag	spalna vreča
sleeping pill	uspavalna tableta
sleepy	zaspan(-a)
slice *(piece of)*	kos
slippers	copati
slope *(mountain)*	pobočje
Slovene *(person)*	Slovenec(-nka)
(language)	slovenščina
slowly	počasi
small	majhen(-hna/-o)
smaller	manjši(-a/-e)
smell *n*	vonj
a bad smell	smrdi
a nice smell	diši
smell *vb*	vohati
smile *n*	nasmešek
smile *vb*	nasmehniti se
smoke *n*	dim
smoke *vb*	kaditi
I don't smoke	ne kadim
smoked *(food)*	prekajen(-a/-o)
smokers *(sign)*	kadilci
smooth	gladek(-dka/-o)
snack	prigrizek
snack bar	okrepčevalnica
snore	smrčati
snow: it's snowing	sneži
snow *n*	sneg

snow chains	snežne verige
snow field	snežišče
snow tyres	zimske gume
soap	milo
soap powder (detergent)	pralni prašek
sober	trezen(-zna/-o)
socks	kratke nogavice
socket	vtičnica
soft	nežen(-žna/-o)
soft drink	brezalkoholna pijača
some	nekaj
someone	nekdo
something	nekaj
sometimes	včasih
son	sin
my son	moj sin
song	pesem
soon	kmalu
sore	vnet(-a/-o)
sorry: I'm sorry!	žal mi je!
soup	juha
south	jug
souvenir	spominek
spa	toplice
spade	lopata
Spain	Španija
spanner	ključ za vijake
spare wheel	rezervno kolo
sparkling: sparkling water	gazirana voda
sparkling wine	peneče vino
spark plug	svečka
speak	govoriti

do you speak English?	govorite angleško?
do you speak German?	govorite nemško?
special	specialen(-lna/-o) ; poseben(-bna/-o)
speciality	specialiteta
speed	hitrost
speed limit	omejitev hitrosti
spell: how do you spell it?	kako se napiše?
spice	pikantna začimba
spicy	pikanten(-tna/-o)
spinach	špinača
spirits (alcohol)	žgane pijače
sponge	goba
spoon	žlica
sport	šport
spring (season)	pomlad
square (in town)	trg
squid	kalamari
stadium	stadion
stairs	stopnice
stalls (in theatre)	parter
stamp	znamka
1 stamp, please	eno znamko, prosim
5 stamps, please	pet znamk, prosim
star	zvezda
start	začetek
starter (in meal)	predjed
(car)	zaganjač
station	postaja
bus station	avtobusna postaja
police station	policijska postaja
train station	železniška postaja

stationer's	papirnica
stay *(reside for while)*	bivati
I'm staying at hotel Slon	sem v hotelu Slon
steak	zrezek
well-done steak	dobro pečen zrezek
rare steak	malo pečen zrezek
medium steak	srednje pečen zrezek
steep	strm(-a/-o)
steering wheel	volan
sterling	angleški funt
stew	enolončnica
steward	stevard
stewardess	stevardesa
sticking plaster	obliž
still: still water	negazirana voda
sting *n*	pik
sting *vb*	pičiti
stomach	trebuh ; želodec
my stomach aches	trebuh me boli
stone	kamen
stop *vb*	ustaviti
stop *(sign)*	stoj
storm	huda nevihta
straight on	naravnost
straw *(for drinking)*	slamica
strawberries	jagode
street	ulica
street map	cestna karta
string	vrvica
strong	močan(-čna/-o)
strong coffee	močna kava
strong tea	močen čaj

student	študent(-ka)
stupid	neumen(-mna/-o)
suddenly	nenadoma
suede	semiš ; velurno usnje
sugar	sladkor
suit	obleka
suitcase	kovček
summer	poletje
summit	vrh
sun	sonce
sunbathe	sončiti se
sunblock	krema za sončenje
sunburn	sončna opeklina
Sunday	nedelja
sunglasses	sončna očala
sunny: it's sunny	sončno je
sunrise	sončni vzhod
sunset	sončni zahod
sunshade	sončnik
sunstroke	sončarica
suntan lotion	krema za sončenje
supermarket	supermarket
supper	večerja
supplement	doplačilo
sure: I'm sure	prepričan(-a) sem
surname	priimek
my surname is…	pišem se
sweater	pulover
sweet adj	sladek(-dka/-o)
sweetener	sladilo
sweets	sladice
swim	plavati

swimming pool	kopališče
swimsuit	kopalna obleka
swing *(for children)*	gugalnica
Swiss cheese	švicarski sir
switch *n*	stikalo
switch off *(light, TV, etc)*	ugasniti
switch on *(light, TV, etc)*	prižgati
Switzerland	Švica
swollen	otekel(-kla/-o)

table	miza
tablecloth	prt
tablespoon	velika žlica
tablet	tableta
table tennis	namizni tenis
table wine	namizno vino
take *vb*	vzeti
talk *vb*	govoriti
tall	visok(-a/-o)
tampons	tamponi
tap	pipa
tape	kaseta
tape recorder	kasetofon
tartar sauce	tatarska omaka
taste *n*	okus
can I taste some?	smem poskusiti?
tax	davek
taxi	taksi
taxi rank	postajališče taksijev

tea	čaj
lemon tea	čaj z limono
tea with milk	čaj z mlekom
strong tea	močen čaj
weak tea	medel čaj
teach	učiti
teacher	učitelj(-ica)
teapot	čajnik
tear *(in material)*	razporek
teaspoon	mala žlička
teeth	zobje
telephone *n*	telefon
by telephone	po telefonu
telephone *vb*	telefonirati
telephone box	telefonska kabina
telephone call	telefonski klic
telephone card	telefonska kartica
telephone directory	telefonski imenik
television	televizija
tell	povedati
temperature	temperatura
I have a temperature	imam temperaturo
temporary	začasno
tennis	tenis
tennis ball	teniška žogica
tennis court	teniško igrišče
tennis racket	teniški lopar
tent	šotor
tent peg	šotorski količek
terrace	terasa
thank you	hvala
thank you very much	najlepša hvala

that one	tisti
theatre	gledališče
there	tam
he's there	tam je
thermometer	termometer
these ones	ti
they	oni ; see GRAMMAR
thick	debel(-a/-o)
(soup)	gost(-a/-o)
thief	tat(-ica)
thigh	bedro
thin	tanek(-nka/-o)
(person)	suh(-a/-o)
thing	stvar
my things	moje stvari
think	misliti
third	tretji(-a/-e)
thirst	žeja
thirsty: I'm thirsty	žejen(-jna) sem
this one	to ; ta
those ones	tisti
thread	sukanec
throat	grlo
thumb	palec
thunderstorm	nevihta
Thursday	četrtek
ticket (train, bus, etc)	vozovnica
1 ticket	ena vozovnica
2 tickets	dve vozovnici
a single ticket	enosmerno vozovnico
a return ticket	povratno vozovnico
(entrance fee)	vstopnina

ticket inspector	kontrolor vozovnic
ticket office	blagajna za prodajo vozovnic
tide *(sea)*	plimovanje
tie	kravata
tights	nogavice
till *n (cash desk)*	blagajna
till *conj (until)*	do
till 2 o'clock	do dveh
till 6 o'clock	do šestih
time *(of day)*	ura
what time is it?	koliko je ura?
do you have time?	imate čas?
timetable	vozni red
tin	konzerva ; pločevinka
tinfoil	staniol
tin-opener	odpirač za konzerve
tiny	majcen(-a/-o)
tip *(waiter, etc)*	napitnina
tired	utrujen(-a)
to	v ; na
to London	v London
to the airport	na letališče
toast *(to eat)*	prepečenec
tobacconist's	trafika
today	danes
toe	prst na nogi
together	skupaj
toilet	stranišče ; WC
toilet paper	toaletni papir
token *(for bus)*	žeton
(for phone)	žeton za telefon
10 tokens	deset žetonov

toll *(motorway)*	cestnina
tomato	paradižnik
tomorrow	jutri
tomorrow morning	jutri zjutraj
tomorrow afternoon	jutri popoldne
tomorrow evening	jutri zvečer
tongue	jezik
tonic water	tonik
tonight	danes zvečer
too	pre…
too hot	prevroče
too noisy	prehrupno
tooth	zob
teeth	zobje
toothache	zobobol
toothbrush	zobna ščetka
toothpaste	zobna pasta
top *adj*: top floor	najvišje nadstropje
top *n*	vrh ; vrhunec
on the top of…	na vrhu…
torch	svetilka
torn	raztrgan(-a/-o)
total	ves ; cel
tough	žilav(-a/-o)
tour	izlet ; tura
tourist	turist
tourist office	turistična agencija
tourist tax	turistična taksa
tourist ticket	turistična vozovnica
tow *vb*	vleči
towel	brisača
tower	stolp

town	mesto
town centre	središče mesta
town hall	rotovž
town plan	plan mesta
toy	igrača
tracksuit	trenirka
traditional	tradicionalen(-lna/-o)
traffic	promet
traffic lights	semafor
train	vlak
the next train	naslednji vlak
the first train	prvi vlak
the last train	zadnji vlak
tram	tramvaj
translate	prevesti
translation	prevod
travel *vb*	potovati
travel agency	turistična agencija
travel sickness	potovalna slabost
traveller's cheques	potovalni čeki
tray	pladenj
tree	drevo
trip	izlet
trousers	hlače
trout	postrv
truck	kamion
trunks *(swimming)*	kopalke
try on *(clothes, shoes)*	pomeriti
T-shirt	majica
Tuesday	torek
tuna	tunina
tunnel	tunel

turkey	puran
turn	obrniti
please turn right	na desno, prosim
please turn left	na levo, prosim
please turn around	obrnite naokrog, prosim
turn off	ugasniti
turn on	prižgati
tweezers	pinceta
twice	dvakrat
twin-bedded room	soba z dvema posteljama
tyre	guma
tyre pressure	pritisk v gumah

umbrella	dežnik
uncle	stric
my uncle	moj stric
uncomfortable	neudoben(-bna/-o)
unconscious	nezavesten(-tna)
under	pod
underpants	spodnje hlače
understand	razumeti
I don't understand	ne razumem
underwear	spodnje perilo
undo	odpeti
unemployed	nezaposlen(-a)
unfasten	odvezati ; razvezati
United States	Združene države Amerike
university	univerza
unleaded petrol	neosvinčeni bencin
unpack *(suitcases)*	izprazniti ; razpakirati

unscrew	odviti
up: to get up	vstati
upstairs	zgoraj
urgently	nujno
use *vb*	uporabljati
useful	koristen(-tna/-o)
usually	običajno ; po navadi
vacancies *(sign)*	proste sobe
no vacancies *(sign)*	zasedeno
valid	veljaven(-vna/-o)
valley	dolina
valuable	dragocen(-a/-o)
van	dostavno vozilo
vase	vaza
veal	teletina
vegetables	zelenjava
vegetarian	vegetarijanec(-nka)
vehicle	prevozno sredstvo
vein	vena
venison	divjačina
very	zelo
vest	majica
video	video
video camera	video kamera
video cassette	vidio kaseta
video recorder	video rekorder
view	razgled
village	vas
vinegar	kis

vineyard	vinograd
visa	viza
visit n	obisk
volleyball	odbojka
voltage	voltaža
vomit vb	bruhati
wage	plača
wait (for)	čakati (na)
waiter(waitress)	natakar(-ica)
waiting room	čakalnica
walk n	hoja
walk vb	hoditi
walking boots	planinski čevlji
walking stick	sprehajalna palica
wall	stena
on the wall	na steni
wallet	denarnica
walnut	oreh
want: I want...	hočem...
we want...	hočemo...
war	vojna
ward (hospital)	oddelek
wardrobe	omara
warm: it's warm	toplo je
wash (body) vb	umiti
(clothes)	prati
(wash oneself)	umiti se
washbasin	umivalnik
washing machine	pralni stroj

washing powder	pralni prašek
wasp	osa
waste bin	koš
watch *n*	ura
watch *vb*	gledati
watchstrap	pas za uro
water	voda
hot water	topla voda
cold water	hladna voda
drinking water	pitna voda
mineral water	mineralna voda
sparkling water	gazirana voda
still water	negazirana voda
waterfall	slap
water heater	bojler za vodo
watermelon	lubenica
water-skiing	smučanje na vodi
wave *vb*	valovati
way	pot ; cesta
way out *(exit)*	izhod
we	mi ; see GRAMMAR
weak coffee	medla kava
weak tea	medel čaj
weather	vreme
wedding	poroka
Wednesday	sreda
week	teden
1 week	en teden
2 weeks	dva tedna
next week	nasllednji teden
last week	prejšnji teden
per week	na teden

weekday	dan v tednu
weekend	konec tedna
weekly	tedenski(-ska/-o)
weight	teža
welcome!	dobrodošli!
well	dobro
he's not well	ni mu dobro
west	zahod
wet	moker(-kra/-o)
what?	kaj?
what is it?	kaj je?
wheel	kolo
wheelchair	invalidski voziček
when?	kdaj?
when is…?	kdaj je…?
where?	kje?
whre is…?	kje je…?
which (one)	kateri(-a/-o)
while: in a while	čez nekaj časa
white	bel(-a/-o)
who?	kdo?
who is it?	kdo je?
whole	cel(-a/-o) ; ves(vsa/vso)
wholemeal	nepresejana moka
whose	čigav(-a/-o)
why?	zakaj?
wide	širok(-a/-o)
wife	žena
my wife	moja žena
wind	veter
window	okno
(of shop)	izložba

windscreen	vetrobran
windscreen wipers	brisalci vetrobrana
windy: it's windy	vetrovno je
wine	vino
red wine	rdeče vino
white wine	belo vino
dry wine	suho vino
sweet wine	sladko vino
rosé wine	rozé vino
sparkling wine	peneče vino
sparkling wine	namizno vino
wine list	vinska karta
winter	zima
with	z ; s
without	brez
without sugar	brez sladkorja
without ice	brez leda
without milk	brez mleka
woman	ženska
wood (substance)	les
woods	gozd
wool	volna
word	beseda
work: it doesn't work	ne deluje
world	svet
worried	zaskrbljen(-a/-o)
worse	slabši(-a/-e)
worth: it's worth...	izplača se
wrap (up)	zaviti
wrapping paper	papir za zavijanje
wrist	zapestje
write	pisati

writing paper	papir za pisanje
wrong *adj*	napačen(-čna/-o)
x-ray *n*	rentgenski žarki
yacht	jahta
year	leto
this year	letos
next year	prihodnje leto
last year	lani
yellow	rumen(-a/-o)
yes	da ; ja
yesterday	včeraj
yet: not yet	ne še
yoghurt	jogurt
you	ti ; vi ; see GRAMMAR
young	mlad(-a/-o)
your	vaš(-a/-e)
your passport	vaš potni list
your room	vaša soba
your bike	vaše kolo
youth hostel	mladinski dom
zero	nič ; nula
zip	zadrga
zone	cona
zoo	živalski vrt

abonmajska karta	season theatre ticket
alergija	allergy
ali	or ; *indicates a question*
ambulanta	outpatients' clinic
amortizer	shock absorber
ananas	pineapple
angleški funt	sterling
Anglež(-inja)	English *(person)*
Anglija	England
apartma	apartment
aretirati	to arrest
artičoka	artichoke
astma	asthma
ata	father
avto	car
avtobus	bus ; coach
avtobusna postaja	bus station ; bus stop
avtocesta	motorway
avtomatičen(-čna/-o)	automatic
avtopralnica	car wash
avtor(-ica)	author

babica	grandmother
balkon	balcony
balon	balloon
bančni račun	bank account
banka	bank
barva	colour
barva za lase	hair dye
baterija	battery

bedro	thigh
bel(-a/-o)	white
bela kava	white coffee
belo meso	white meat
beležka	note pad
beležka z naslovi	address book
belilo	bleach
beljakova pena	meringue
beluš	asparagus
bencin	petrol
bencinska črpalka	petrol station
bife	buffet ; snack bar
blagajna	cash desk ; till
blazina	pillow ; cushion
blažilec	shock absorber
blisk	flash
blizu	near
bluza	blouse
bog	God
bogat(-a/-o)	rich (person)
bohinj	hard sheep's-milk cheese
bolan(-na/-o)	sick ; ill
boleč(-a/-e)	painful
bolečina	pain
boleti	to ache ; to hurt
bolje (kot)	better (than)
bolnišnica	hospital
bombaž	cotton
božič	Christmas
božični večer	Christmas Eve
brat	brother
bravina	mutton

breskev	peach
brez	without
brezalkoholen(-lna/-o)	non-alcoholic
brezplačen(-čna/-o)	free of charge
brisača	towel
Britanija	Britain
briti	to shave
britvice	razor blades
brivec	barber
brivski aparat	razor
brošura	brochure
bucika	pin
budilka	alarm clock
bunda	ski jacket
carina	customs ; duty ; tariff
cel(-a/-o)	whole ; all ; total
cena	price
ceneje	cheaper
cenik	price list
cerkev	church
cesta	street ; road
cestna karta	road map ; street plan
cev	pipe ; tube
cigarete	cigarettes
cmoki	dumplings
marelični cmoki	apricot dumplings
sirovi cmoki	cheese dumplings
cona	zone
copati	slippers

cvetača	cauliflower
cvetica	flower
čaj	tea
čaj z limono	lemon tea
čaj z mlekom	tea with milk
čakalnica	waiting room
čakati v vrsti	to queue
čas	time
časopis	newspaper
čebula	onion
češnja	cherry
ček	cheque
čekovna knjižica	cheque book
čep	plug (for sink)
česen	garlic
čestitke	congratulations
četrtek	Thursday
čevapčiči	rolls filled with mince
čevelj	shoe
čevlji	shoes
čipka	lace (material)
čips	crisps
čist(-a/-o)	clean
čista juha	clear soup
čistilnica	dry-cleaner's
član	member (of club, etc)
članarina	membership fee
članek	article
čokolada	chocolate
čokoladni bomboni	chocolates

čokoladno mleko	**cocoa**
čoln	**boat**
čoln na vesla	**rowing boat**
čolnarjenje	**boating ; sailing**
čolnarna	**boathouse**
čopič	**brush** (for painting)
črka	**letter** (of alphabet)
črn(-a/-o)	**black**
črna kava	**black coffee**
črni kruh	**brown bread**
čutara	**flask**
da	**yes**
daleč	**far**
dan	**day**
dan v tednu	**weekday**
danes	**today**
darilo	**gift**
dati	**to give**
dati nazaj	**to give back**
dati v najem	**to let** (property)
datum	**date**
datum rojstva	**date of birth**
davek	**tax**
debel(-a/-o)	**fat ; thick**
dekle	**girl**
dekliško ime	**maiden name**
del	**part**
delati	**to work ; to do**
delikatese	**delicatessen**

deliti	to share
denar	money
denarnica	purse ; wallet
desert	dessert
destilirana voda	distilled water
dete	baby
dež	rain
dežela	country
dežnik	umbrella
dežni plašč	raincoat
dijeta	diet
direktni vlak	direct train
direktor	manager
diesel	diesel
divjačina	game *(meat)*
dneven(-vna/-o)	daily
dnevna soba	living room ; lounge
do	till ; until
dober(-bra/-o)	good
dober dan	good afternoon ; good day
dober večer	good evening
dobro jutro	good morning
dobiti	to get
dobro	well
dobrodošli!	welcome!
dokumenti	documents
dol	down
iti dol	to go down
dolar	dollar
dolenjski cviček	type of red wine from Dolenjska
dolg(-a/-o)	long
dolina	valley

dom	home
dopoldne	in the morning
doplačilo	supplement
dopust	holiday
na dopustu	on holiday
dovoliti	to permit
dovolj	enough
drag(-a/-o)	dear ; expensive
dragocen(-a/-o)	valuable
drevo	tree
driska	diarrhoea
drobiž	change *(small coins)*
drsanje	skating
drugačen(-čna/-o)	different
drugi(-a/-o)	other ; second
družina	family
država	country *(nation)*
državljan(-ka)	citizen
državljanstvo	nationality
državna meja	national frontier
duhovnik	priest
Dunaj	Vienna
duty-free trgovina	duty-free shop
dvakrat	twice
dvigalo	lift ; elevator
dvojen	double
dvopasovna cesta	dual carriageway
dvoposteljna soba	double room
dvorana	hall
džem	jam

eden ; en	one
ekskurzija	excursion
elastika	elastic band
elektrika	electricity
električen(-čna/-o)	electric
element	cupboard
enkrat	once
enolončnica	stew
enoposteljna soba	single room
enosmerna cesta	one-way road
enosmerna vozovnica	one-way ticket
etiketa	label
Euroček	Eurocheque
Evropa	Europe
evropski(-a/-o)	European

februar	February
fazan	pheasant
fant	boy ; boyfriend
fen	hair dryer
fige	figs
filigran	filigree
firma	company ; firm
fižol	beans
fižolova juha	bean soup
fotoaparat	camera
fotografija	photograph
fotokopirati	to photocopy
Francija	France
francoski kruh	French bread

Francoz(-inja)	**French** (person)
frizer	**hairdresser**
funt	**pound** (money)
galerija	**gallery**
garaža	**garage**
garderoba	**cloakroom ; left-luggage office**
gasilci	**fire brigade**
glas	**voice**
glasba	**music**
glava	**head**
glavni(-vna/-o)	**main**
glavna jed	**main course**
glavno mesto	**capital city**
glavnik	**comb**
glavobol	**headache**
gledališče	**theatre**
gledališka blagajna	**box office** (theatre)
gledati	**to watch**
globok	**deep**
gluh(-a)	**deaf**
gnil(-a/-o)	**rotten** (fruit, etc)
gobe	**mushrooms**
gobova juha	**mushroom soup**
gondola	**cable-car** (cable-car)
gora	**mountain**
gorčica	**mustard**
goreti	**to burn**
gorivo	**fuel**
gos	**goose**

gospa	Mrs ; Ms
gospod	Mr ; sir
gospodična	Miss
gospodinja	housekeeper (female)
gost	guest
gost(-a/-o)	thick (soup) ; heavy (traffic)
gostilna	inn
gostišče	inn
gotovina	ready cash
govedina	beef
goveja obara	beef stew
goveja pečenka	roast beef
goveji golaž	beef goulash
govoriti	to speak ; to talk
gozd	forest
grad	castle
graditi	to build
grah	peas
gram	gramme
gramofonska plošča	record (music)
grenek(-nka/-o)	bitter
grenivka	grapefruit
gretje	heating
grič	hill
gripa	flu
grlo	throat
grob	grave
grozdje	grapes
gugalnica	swing (for children)
guma	rubber
gumb	button

hči	daughter
higienski vložki	sanitary towels
hiša	house
hišna lastnica	landlady
hišni lastnik	landlord
hiter(-tra/-o)	fast ; quick
hitro	quickly
hitrost	speed
hlače	trousers
hladen(-dna/-o)	cool ; cold
hladilna naprava	air-conditioning
hladilna torba	cool box
hladilnik	fridge
hlebec	loaf
hlebec kruha	a loaf of bread
hobotnica	octopus
hoja v hribih	hill-walking
hoja	walk
hrana	food
hrana za otroka	baby food
hrapav(-a/-o)	rough
hrbet	back
hrib	hill
hrup	noise
hruška	pear
hruške	pears
Hrvat(-ica)	Croatian *(person)*
Hrvatska	Croatia
huda nevihta	storm
huda paprika	chilli
hudoben(-bna/-o)	nasty ; bad
hvala	thank you

igra	game
igrača	toy
igralnica	playroom ; casino
igrati	to play
igrišče	recreation ground
igrišče za golf	golf course
ime	first name
imeti	to have
in	and
injekcija	injection
informacije	information office ; enquiries
informacijski urad	enquiry office
instant kava	instant coffee
invalid	disabled person
invalidski voziček	wheelchair
iskati	to look for
isti	same
iti	to go ; see GRAMMAR
iti dol	to go down
iti nazaj	go back
iti noter	go in
iti po	to fetch
iti ven	go out
iz	from ; of
izdatek	expense
izdelek	product
izgubiti	to lose
izgubljen(-a/-o)	lost
izgubljeni predmeti	lost property
izhod	exit
izklopiti	to switch off
izlet	trip

izlet z avtobusom	bus tour ; coach trip
izlet z ladjo	boat trip
izpit	examination
izpolniti	to fill in
izpolnite ta formular	fill in this form
izpušna cev	exhaust pipe
izstopiti	to get off
izvir	spring ; source of river
ja	yes
jabolčni sok	apple juice
jabolčni zavitek	apple strudel
jabolčnik	cider
jabolko	apple
jadrati	sailing
jadrnica	sailing boat
jagnje	lamb
jagoda	strawberry
jahati	to ride *(horse)*
jahta	yacht
jajce	egg
mehko kuhano jajce	soft-boiled egg
pečeno jajce	fried egg
trdo kuhano jajce	hard-boiled egg
jama	cave
jamstvo	guarantee
januar	January
jastog	lobster
javen(-vna/-o)	public
jaz	I ; see GRAMMAR

je	is ; see GRAMMAR
jed	meal ; dish
jedilnica	dining room
jedilni list	menu
jedilni pribor	cutlery
jegulja	eel
jesen	autumn
jesti	to eat ; see GRAMMAR
jetra	liver
jezero	lake
jezik	tongue ; language
jogurt	yoghurt
jopa	cardigan
jota	potato, bean and cabbage soup
jug	south
juha	soup
julij	July
junij	June
jutri	tomorrow
jutro	morning
jugovzhoden(-dna/-o)	southeastern
jugozahoden(-dna/-o)	southwestern
kabina za preoblačenje	changing room
kadilci	smokers
kaditi prepovedano	no smoking
kaj	any ; what?
kajenje prepovedano	no smoking
kako?	how?
kalamari	squid

kam?	where to?
kamp	camp
kamping	campsite
kanu	canoe
kapa	cap
kapela	chapel
karafa	carafe
karavana	caravan
karkoli	anything
karta	ticket ; map
kaseta	cassette ; tape
kasetofon	tape recorder
kašljati	to cough
kasneje	later
katedrala	cathedral
kateri(-a/-o)	which one
kava	coffee
kava brez kafeina	decaffeinated coffee
kavarna	café
kazen	fine *(penalty)*
kdaj?	when?
kdo?	who?
keksi	biscuits
kilogram	kilogram
kilometer	kilometre
kino	cinema
kip	sculpture
kis	vinegar
kisla kumarica	pickled gherkin
kje?	where?
kladivo	hammer
klešče	pliers

klin	peg
ključ	key
ključ za vijake	spanner
ključavnica	lock
klobasa	sausage
klobuk	hat
klub	club
kmalu	soon
kmečki turizem	farm tourism
kmetija	farm
knjiga	book
knjigarna	bookshop
knjigovodja(knjigovodkinja)	accountant
knjižica	booklet
knjižnica	library
koča	mountain hut
koka-kola®	Coke®
kokosov oreh	coconut
kokošja juha	chicken soup
koledar	calendar
koledarček	diary
koleno	knee
kolesariti	to cycle
kolesarska steza	cycle route
koliko	how many? ; how much?
kolo	bicycle ; wheel
komar	mosquito
kompas	compass
komplet za prvo pomoč	first-aid kit
končati	to finish
koncert	concert
kondom	condom

konec	end
konec tedna	weekend
konferenca	conference
konj	horse
konkurent(-ka)	competitor
kontracepcija	contraceptive
kontrola	checkpoint
kontrolirati	to check
kontrolor vozovnic	ticket inspector
konzerva	tin ; can
konzulat	consulate
kopališče	swimming pool
kopalke	swimming trunks
kopalna kapa	bathing cap
kopalna obleka	swimming costume
kopalnica	bathroom
kopel	bath
kopija	print *(photo)* ; copy
korenje	carrots
kos	piece ; slice
kos kruha	a slice of bread
koš	waste bin
košara	basket
košarka	basketball
kosilo	lunch
kositer	pewter
kostanj	chestnut
kovanec	coin
kovček	suitcase
kozarec	glass *(for drinking)*
kozarec vode	a glass of water
kozmetika	make-up

kralj	king
kraljevski(-ska/-o)	royal
kraljica	queen
kraj	spot ; point ; village
krap	carp ; fritter
kraški teran	type of red wine from Karst
kraška jama	Karst cave
kratek(-tka/-o)	short
kratke nogavice	socks
kratke hlače	shorts
krava	cow
kravata	tie
kreditna kartica	credit card
krema	cream *(lotion)*
krema za britje	shaving cream
krema za čevlje	shoe-polish
krema za sončenje	suntan lotion
kri	blood
krilo	skirt
križarjenje	cruise
križišče	junction
krompir	potato
pire krompir	mashed potatoes
maslen krompir	sauté potatoes
pražen krompir	fried potatoes with onions
krožnik	plate
krtača	brush
krtača za lase	hairbrush
kruh	bread
krvna skupina	blood group
kuhinja	kitchen
kumara	cucumber

kupe	compartment *(train)*
kupiti	to buy
kura	chicken
ocvrta kura	chicken fried in breadcrumbs
pečena kura	roast chicken
kurja juha	chicken soup
kurja obara	chicken stew
kvaliteta	quality
ladja	ship
lahek(-hka/-o)	easy
lahko	to be able to
lahko noč	good night
lak za nohte	nail polish
lakota	hunger
lasje	hair
lastnik	owner
leča	lentils
leče	contact lenses
led	ice
poškodovan(-a/-o)	injured
pošta	post office
poštna številka	postcode
poštni nabiralnik	postbox ; letterbox
ledvice	kidneys
lekarna	chemist's
lep(-a/-o)	beautiful
lepilni trak	Sellotape®
lepilo	glue
les	wood *(substance)*

lešnik (kiki-riki)	peanut
lestev	ladder
letališče	airport
letalo	plane
letalska pošta	air mail
leteti	to fly
letina	harvest
leto	year
letovišče	summer holiday resort
levo	left
ležalnik	deck chair
licitacija	auction
lignji	squid
likalnik	iron (for clothes)
limona	lemon
limonada	lemonade
list	leaf (tree) ; sheet (paper)
liter	litre
ljubek(-bka/-o)	pretty ; lovely
ljubezniv(-a/-o)	kind
ljubiti	to love
ljudje	people
ločen(-a)	divorced ; separated
lomljiv(-a/-o)	breakable
lončarstvo	pottery
lonec	pot (for cooking)
lopar	racket (tennis etc)
teniški lopar	tennis racket
lopata	spade
losos	salmon
lubenica	watermelon
luknja	hole

luknjica	puncture
luksuz	luxury
luna park	funfair
lutka	doll
lutkovna igra	puppet show
maček	cat
maj	May
majhen(-hna/-o)	small
majica	T-shirt ; vest
malina	raspberry
malinovec	raspberry syrup
malo	little ; a bit
mama	mother
mandelj	almond
manj	less
manjkajoč(-a/-e)	missing (thing)
marec	March
marelica	apricot
marelice	apricots
margarina	margarine
marmelada	jam
marmor	marble
maša	mass (church)
maslo	butter
mavrica	rainbow
mazilo	ointment
med	honey
medeni tedni	honeymoon
medicina	medicine

medicinska sestra	nurse
mednarodni(-a/-o)	international
mednarodni menji prehod	international border crossing
mednarodno letališče	international airport
meduza	jellyfish
megla	fog
mehanik	mechanic
meja	**border** (of country)
melancana	aubergine
melona	melon
menjalni tečaj	exchange rate
menjalnica	bureau de change
menstruacija	**period** (menstruation)
mesec	month
mesnica	butcher's
meso	meat
mestna hiša	town hall
mesto	city ; town
meter	metre
mi	we ; see GRAMMAR
midva	we two ; see GRAMMAR
migrena	migraine
mikrovalovna pečica	microwave oven
milijon	million
milimeter	millimetre
milo	soap
milo v prahu	soap powder
mineralna voda	mineral water
minuta	minute
miš	mouse
miza	table
mlad(-a/-o)	**young** (person)

mladinski dom	youth hostel
mleko	milk
mleko v prahu	powdered milk
mleto meso	minced meat
mlin na veter	windmill
mnogo	many
množica	crowd ; mass *(a lot)*
močan(-čna/-o)	strong
moda	fashion
moder(-dra/-o)	blue
moka	flour
moker(-kra/-o)	wet
morda	maybe ; perhaps
morje	sea
morska bolezen	seasickness
morski sadeži	seafood
morski rakec	shrimp
MOŠKI	Gents' *(toilet)*
most	bridge
motnja	disturbance ; interference
motor	motor ; engine
motorni čoln	motorboat
motorno kolo	motorcycle
mož	husband ; man
možgani	brain
mrčes	insect
mrtev(-tva/-o)	dead
mrzel(-zla/-o)	cold
mucek	kitten
muzej	museum
muzejski vlak	historical railway

na	onto ; on ; to ; per
na desno	to the right
na levo	to the left
na svidenje	goodbye
na uro	per hour
nadevan puran	stuffed turkey
nadstropje	floor
najvišje nadstropje	top floor
nag(-a/-o)	naked
nagelj	carnation
nagrada	prize ; award
nahrbtnik	rucksack
najboljši(-a/-e)	best
najemnina	rental
najeti	to hire
najlepša hvala	thank you very much
najljubši(-bša/-e)	favourite
najti	to find
najvišja cena	peak rate
najvišje nadstropje	top floor
nakit	jewellery
nakupovalno središče	shopping centre
namesto	instead
namizni tenis	table tennis
napačen(-čna/-o)	wrong
napad	attack ; fit
napaka	flaw ; error
napitnina	tip *(waiter, etc)*
naplačilo	deposit
napolniti	to fill up
napoved	forecast
naprava za gašenje ognja	fire extinguisher

naprej	forwards
naravna znamenitost	(site of) natural beauty
naravnost	straight on
naroden(-dna/-no)	national
narodni park	national park
naslednji(-a/-e)	next
naslov	address ; title (book, film etc)
nasproti	opposite
natakar	waiter
natakarica	waitress
navada	custom (tradition) ; habit
navadno	usually
nazaj	backward(s)
ne	no ; not
nebo	sky
nečak	nephew
nečakinja	niece
nedelja	Sunday
nedrček	bra
negativ	negative (photography)
nekadilci	non-smokers
nekaj	some ; any
nekdo	someone
Nemčija	Germany
Nemec(-mka)	German (person)
nemogoč(-a/-e)	impossible
nenadoma	suddenly
neposreden(-dna/-o)	direct
nepresejana moka	wholemeal
nesreča	accident
neudoben(-bna/-o)	uncomfortable
nevaren(-rna/-o)	dangerous

nevarnost	danger
nevihta	storm (rain)
nezaposlen(-a)	unemployed
nezavesten(-tna)	unconscious
nežen(-žna/-o)	soft
nič	zero ; nothing
nihče	nobody ; none
nikoli	never
nizek(-zka/-o)	low
noč	night
nočni klub	nightclub
noga	leg ; foot
nogavice	tights
nogomet	football
noht	nail (on finger)
norice	chickenpox
nos	nose
noseča	pregnant
nositi	to carry ; to wear (clothes)
notri	inside
nov(-a/-o)	new
novo leto	New Year
nož	knife
nujnost	emergency
nula	zero
o	about
ob	by ; at ; near
oba	both
obala	coast

obalna straža	coastguard
obara	stew
goveja obara	beef stew
kurja obara	chicken stew
obdržati	to keep
obešalnik	coat hanger
obesek za ključe	keyring
običajno	usually
obisk	visit
oblak	cloud
obleči se	to dress (oneself)
obleka	man's suit ; woman's dress
obleke	clothes
obliž	sticking plaster
območje	area
obnašati se	to behave
obraz	face
obrniti	to turn
obroč na kolesu	tyre
obveza	bandage
obvezen(-zna/-o)	compulsory
obvoz	bypass ; detour
očala	glasses
oče	father
oči	eyes
očim	stepfather
ocvrt(-a/-o)	fried
od	from ; of
od kod?	from where?
odbojka	volleyball
odčepnik	corkscrew
oddelek	department

odeja	duvet ; blanket
odhodi	departures
oditi	to leave
odličen(-čna/-o)	perfect ; excellent
odpadki	litter *(rubbish)*
odpeljati	to leave *(by car)*
odpeti	to undo
odpirač za steklenice	bottle opener
odpirač za konzerve	tin-opener
odporen(-rna/-o)	resistant
odpovedati	to cancel
odpreti	to open
odprt(-a/-o)	open
odrasel(-sla/-slo)	adult
odškodnina	refund
odvetnik(-ica)	lawyer ; solicitor
odvezati	to unfasten
odviti	to unscrew
ogenj	fire
ogled z vodičem	guided tour
ogledalo	mirror
ognjemet	fireworks
ogrlica	necklace
okno	window
oko	eye
okoli	about ; around
okolica	surroundings
okrasiti	to decorate
okrepčevalnica	snack bar
okrogel(-gla/-o)	round
okus	flavour
okvara na motorju	breakdown *(car)*

oliva	olive
olivno olje	olive oil
olje	oil
omaka	sauce ; gravy
omara	wardrobe
omarica	**locker** *(for luggage)*
omejitev hitrosti	speed limit
omleta	omelette
omleta s sirom	cheese omelette
omleta s šunko	ham omelette
on	he ; see GRAMMAR
ona	she ; see GRAMMAR
onadva	they two ; see GRAMMAR
onesnaženje	pollution
oni	they ; see GRAMMAR
opatija	abbey
opoldan	midday
opoldne	at midday
opozorilo!	warning!
oprostite!	excuse me!
oprema	equipment
optična leča	lens
oranžen(-žna/-o)	orange
orehi	walnuts
osa	wasp
osebje	staff
osebna izkalnica	identity card
oseka	low tide
ošpice	measles
osrednji(-a/-e)	central
ostati	to stay
ostriga	oyster

otok	island
otrok	child
otroci	children
otroški stolček	high chair
ovca	sheep
ovinek	turning ; bend
ozek(-zka/-o)	narrow
ozka ulica	narrow street ; alley

pahljača	fan *(hand-held)*
palača	palace
palačinke	pancakes
panoramska železnica	scenic railway
papir	paper
papir za pisanje	writing paper
papir za zavijanje	wrapping paper
papirnica	stationer's
par	pair
paradižnik	tomato
paradižnikova juha	tomato soup
paradižnikova solata	tomato salad
parfum	perfume
park	park
parkirati	to park
parkirni prostor	parking space
parkirišče	car park
parkirna ura	parking disc
parter	stalls *(in theatre)*
pas	belt ; waist
pašteta	paté

pasti	to fall
paziti	to look after
pečen(-a/-o)	fried ; baked
pečen na žaru	grilled
pečica	oven
pecivo	pastry
pek	baker
pekarna	baker's
peljati	to drive
peneč(-a/-e)	sparkling
penzion	guesthouse
perilo	underwear
pero	pen
peron	platform *(railway)*
perutnina	poultry
pes	dog
pesa	beetroot
pešec	pedestrian
peš pot	footpath
petek	Friday
peteršilj	parsley
pičiti	to sting
pijača	drink
pijan(-a)	drunk
pik	bite *(insect)*
pikanten(-tna/-o)	spicy
piknik	picnic
pilula	pill
pipa	tap ; pipe *(for smoking)*
pisarna	office
pisati	to write
pismo	letter

piščanec	chicken
pita	pie
piti	to drink
pitna voda	drinking water
pivo	beer
pižama	pyjamas
plačano	paid
plačati	to pay
plačilo	payment
plan mesta	town plan
planine	mountains
planinska koča	climbing boots
planinski čevlji	climbing boots
plašč	coat
plastičen(-čna/-o)	plastic
plavalni bazen	swimming pool
plavati	to swim
plavuti	flippers
plaz	avalanche
plaža	beach
plenica	nappy
ples	dance
plešast	bald *(person)*
plesati	to dance
pletena jopica	sweater
plezati	to climb
plima	high tide
plin	gas
plitev(-tva/-o)	shallow
pločevinka	can *(drinks)* ; tin
pločnik	pavement
po	after ; on ; by

pobegniti	to escape
počasen(-sna/-o)	slow
počasi	slowly
poceni	cheap
počitnice	holidays
počivati	to rest
pod	under
podeželska cesta	country lane (road)
podoben(-bna/-o)	similar
podpis	signature
podrobnosti	details
področje	area
področje kmečkega turizma	farm tourism area
podružnica	branch (of business, etc.)
podzemen(-mna/-o)	underground
pogost(-a/-o)	frequent
pogosto	often
pogrešan(-a/-o	missing
pohištvo	furniture
pokazati	to show
poklicati	to call
pokopališče	cemetery
pokvarjen(-a/-o)	rotten (milk, food, etc)
pokvarjen(-a/-o)	broken down
pol	half
pol steklenice ...	a half bottle of ...
polet	flight
polica	shelf
polica za prtljago	luggage rack
policija	police
policijska postaja	police station
policist	police officer

polje	field
poljub	kiss
poln(-a/-o)	full ; crowded
polni penzion	full board
polnoč	midnight
polovica	half
polovična cena	half-price
pomagati	to help
pomaranča	orange
pomarančna marmelada	marmalade
pomarančni sok	orange juice
pomemben(-bna/-o)	important
pomeriti	to try on *(clothes, shoes)*
pomes frittes	chips
pomivalni stroj	dishwasher
pomlad	spring
pomoč	help ; aid ; assistance
pomol	pier
ponedeljek	Monday
ponovno napolniti	to refill
ponudba	offer
poper	pepper *(spice)*
poplava	flood
popoldan	afternoon
popoldne	in the afternoon
popraviti	to repair
popust	discount
poročen(-a)	married
poroka	wedding
poseben(-bna/-o)	special
posebno zanimiv objekt	site of exceptional interest
posel	business

poslati	to post ; to send
poslušati	to listen to
posneto mleko	skimmed milk
pospeševalec	accelerator
postaja	station
postajališče taksijev	taxi rank
postelja	bed
postelja za eno osebo	single bed
zakonska postelja	double bed
posteljnina	bedding
postrešček	porter
postrežba	service
postrežba je vračunana	service included
postrežba v sobi	room service
postrv	trout
posušiti	to dry
poškodovan(-a/-o)	injured
pošta	post office
poštna številka	postcode
poštni nabiralnik	postbox ; letterbox
pot	way ; path
poteči	to expire ; to end
potegni!	pull
potica	nut cake
potni list	passport
potnik(-ica)	passenger
potok	stream
potovalni čeki	traveller's cheques
potovanje	journey
potovati	to travel
potovati z avtoštopom	to hitchhike
potrdilo	confirmation

potrditi	to confirm
potreben(-bna/-o)	necessary
povabilo	invitation
povračilo	refund
povratna vozovnica	return ticket
pozabiti	to forget
pozdravljeni	hello
pozen(-zna/-o)	late
prah	dust
pralni stroj	washing machine
pralni prašek	washing powder
pralnica	launderette
pralno sredstvo	detergent
prašek proti mrčesu	insect powder
prati	to wash
prav	OK ; right
pravila	rules ; regulations
pravilen(-lna/-o)	correct ; right
prazen(-zna/-o)	blank ; empty
prazna guma	flat tyre
praznik	public holiday
prečna cesta	crossroads
pred	ago ; before
pred hotelom	in front of the hotel
predal	drawer
preden	before
predjed	starter (in meal)
predpisi	instructions ; regulations
predstava	performance ; show
prehod	crossing
prehod čez želnico	level crossing
prehod za pešce	pedestrian crossing

prej	before
prejšnji(-a/-e)	former
prekajen(-a/-o)	smoked *(meat)*
prekmurska gibanica	nut/apple/cream-cheese cake
preko	over
prenočišče	accommodation
preobleči se	to change clothes
prepečenec	toast *(to eat)*
prepisati	to copy
prepovedan(-a/-o)	prohibited
preprost(-a/-o)	simple
presežek	excess ; surplus
prestava	gear *(on car)*
pretres	shock
preveč	too much
prevesti	to translate
previden(-dna/-o)	careful
prevleka za blazino	pillowcase
prevod	translation
prevozno sredstvo	vehicle
prha	shower
pri	by ; at
prihod	arrival
prihodi	arrivals
prikuhe	side dishes
priimek	surname
prijatelj-ica	friend
prijava	check-in
prijaviti	to declare
prijavljen(-a/-o)	registered
prijeten(-tna/-o)	pleasant ; nice
prilagoditi	to adjust ; to adapt

priljubljen(-a/-o)	popular
primerjati	to compare
princ	prince
princesa	princess
prinesti	to bring
pripomočki	facilities
prispeti	to arrive
pristan	quay
pristanek	landing *(of plane)*
pristanišče	harbour ; port *(sea)*
pritožba	complaint
priti	to come
pritisk v gumah	tyre pressure
pritličje	ground floor
pritožiti se	to complain
privatno	private
prižgati	to switch on
prodati ; prodajati	to sell
program	programme
promet	traffic
prosim	please
prosto	vacant
prostor	place ; space
proti	against ; for
proti predpisom	against the rules
tablete proti glavobolu	tablets for a headache
prstan	ring *(for fingers)*
pršut	cured ham from Karst
prtljaga	luggage
prvi(-a/-o)	first
prva pomoč	first aid
prvo nadstropje	first floor

ptica	bird
pulover	pullover
pult	counter *(shops, bar etc)*
puran	turkey
nadevan puran	stuffed turkey
raca	duck
račun	bill ; receipt ; invoice
računalnik	computer
rad(a) imeti	to like
raje (imeti)	to prefer
rakovica	crab
raven(-vna/-o)	flat
razbiti	to break
razdalja	distance
razen	except
razgled	view
razgledna točka	viewpoint
razglednica	postcard
razkužilo	disinfectant ; antiseptic
razložiti	to explain
razmerje	rate
razprodaja	sales
razstava	exhibition ; display
razumeti	to understand
razvedrilo	entertainment
razviti	to develop
ražnjiči	shish kebab
rdeč(-a/-e)	red
recepcija	reception *(desk)*

recept	prescription ; recipe *(cooking)*
reči	to say
redek(-dka/-o)	rare
redkev	radish
reka	river
resen(-sna/-o)	serious
rešiti	to rescue
rešilni avto	ambulance
rešilni pas	lifeboat
restavracija	restaurant
reven(-vna/-o)	poor
revija	magazine
revma	rheumatism
rezervacija	booking ; reservation
rezervirati	to reserve ; to book
rezervno kolo	spare wheel
rezina	slice
riba	fish
ribariti	to fish
ribez	currant
ribiška mreža	fishing net
ribji zrezek	fish fillet
rini!	push
risanje	drawing
riž	rice
riž z gobami	rice with mushrooms
riž z grahom	rice with peas
rjav(-a/-e)	brown
rjuha	sheet *(for bed)*
rob	edge
robec	handkerchief
ročna prtljaga	hand luggage

ročna torbica	**handbag**
ročno izdelan	**handmade**
rojstni dan	**birthday**
rojstni list	**birth certificate**
roka	**hand ; arm**
rokavice	**gloves**
rokodelec	**craftsman**
rolo	**shutters**
Rotovž	**Town Hall**
roza	**pink**
roža	**plant ; flower**
rozina	**raisin**
rudnik	**mine**
rumen(-a/-e)	**yellow**
ruta	**scarf**
rženi kruh	**rye bread**

s	**with**
sadna kupa	**fruit salad**
sadje	**fruit**
sadni sok	**fruit juice**
salama	**salami**
sam(-a)	**alone**
samski	**bachelor**
samska	**single woman** *(unmarried)*
samo	**only**
samopostrežna	**self-service** *(shop)*
samostan	**monastery**
samski(-ska)	**single** *(not married)*
sandali	**sandals**

sardine	sardines
sedaj	now
sedeti	to sit
sedeti spredaj	to sit in front *(in car)*
sedeti zadaj	to sit in the back *(in car)*
sedež	seat
sedežnica	ski-lift *(chair-lift)*
sejem	fair
sekunda	second *(time)*
semafor	traffic lights
semiš	suede
sendvič	sandwich
sesalec	vacuum cleaner
sestavine	ingredients
sestra	sister
sever	north
sidro	anchor
sin	son
sir	cheese
S.I.T.	*abbrev.* Tolar
siv(-a/-e)	grey
skodelica	cup
skoraj	almost
skozi	through
skupaj	together
skupina	group ; band *(musical etc)*
slab(-a/-e)	bad
slaba prebava	indigestion
slaboten(-tna/-o)	weak ; frail
sladek(-dka/-o)	sweet
sladica	pudding ; sweet
sladkor	sugar

sladoled	ice cream
slamica	straw (for drinking)
slanina	bacon
slap	waterfall
slasten(-tna/-o)	delicious
slaven(-vna/-o)	famous
slediti	to follow
slep	blind (person)
slika	picture (on wall)
slišati	to hear
sliva	plum
slovar	dictionary
slušalka	headphones
slušni aparat	hearing aid
služba	job
smer	direction ; route
smetana	cream (on milk)
smeti	rubbish
smetnjak	bin (dustbin)
smokva	fig
smučanje na vodi	water-skiing
smučarska palica	ski-pole
smučarska vlečnica	ski-lift (drag-lift)
sneg	snow
soba	room
dvoposteljna soba	double room
enoposteljna soba	single room
soba z dvema posteljama	twin room
sobota	Saturday
sok	juice ; squash
pomarančni sok	orange juice
jabolčni sok	apple juice

sol	salt
solata	salad
mešana solata	mixed salad
sezonska solata	salad of the season
mešana solata	mixed salad
zelena solata	green salad
sončarica	sunstroke
sonce	sun
sončen(-čna/-o)	sunny
sončiti se	sunbathe
sončna očala	sunglasses
sončna opeklina	sunburn
sončni vzhod	sunrise
sončni zahod	sunset
soprog	partner *(friend)*
sosed(-a)	neighbour
spalna vreča	sleeping bag
spalna srajca	nightdress
spalnica	bedroom
spalnik	sleeper *(on train)*
spati	to sleep
spodaj	down ; downstairs
spodnje hlače	underpants ; knickers
spodnje perilo	underwear
spomenik	monument
spominek	souvenir
spominki	souvenirs
sporočilo	message ; information
sprejemenljiv(-a/-o)	acceptable
sprejeti	to accept
sprevodnik	conductor *(on bus)*
sprostiti se	to relax

Slovene	English
spust po hitrih vodah	white-water rafting
srajca	shirt
srce	heart
srebro	silver
sreča	luck
srečanje	meeting
sreda	Wednesday
središče	centre
središče mesta	town centre
stadion	stadium
staniol	foil (silver)
stanovanje	flat
stanovati	to live
star(-a/-o)	old
stara mama	grandmother
starejši občani	senior citizens
stari oče	grandfather
starine	antiques ; second-hand goods
starost	age
starši	parents
stavba	building
steklenica	bottle
steklina	rabies
stena	wall
stevard	steward
stevardesa	stewardess
steza	path
stikalo	switch
stojnica	market stall
stol	chair
stoletje	century
stolnica	cathedral

stolp	tower
stopnice	stairs
stotin	*Slovene unit of currency*
stranišče	toilet
stranka	client ; customer ; political party
stranska cesta	minor road
stražar	guard
strm(-a/-o)	steep
stroj	machine ; engine
strop	ceiling
strošek	expense
strupen(-a/-o)	poisonous
studenec	fountain
suh(-a/-o)	dry ; thin *(person)*
suha sliva	prune
suknjič	jacket
sulec	salmon
surovo maslo	butter
suša	drought
sušiti	to dry
sveča	candle
svečka	spark plug
svet	world
svetilka	lamp ; torch
svetloba	light
svež(-a/-e)	fresh
sveže postrvi	fresh trout
svila	silk
svinjina	pork
svinjska pečenka	roast pork
svinjski kotlet	pork chop
svoboden(-dna/-o)	free

šal	**shawl ; scarf** *(wool)*
šampanjec	**champagne**
šampon	**shampoo**
ščetka	**brush**
še	**more ; another**
še eden	**another one**
še kruha	**more bread**
širok(-a/-o)	**wide**
šivanka	**needle**
škarje	**scissors**
škatla	**box**
škoda	**harm ; damage**
školjke	**shellfish**
škornji	**boots**
Škotska	**Scotland**
šola	**school**
šotor	**tent**
šotorski količek	**tent peg**
špecerija	**grocer's**
špageti	**spaghetti**
špinača	**spinach**
šport	**sport**
športni center	**sports centre**
št.	*abbrev. for* **številka**
števec	**meter**
številka	**number ; size** *(for clothes, shoes)*
študent(-ka)	**student**
študentska izkanica	**student card**
štruklji	**pastry roulade with sweet and savoury fillings**
šunka	**ham**
švicarski sir	**Swiss cheese**

ta	this
tableta	tablet
tajnik(-ica)	secretary
tako	so
takoj	immediately
taksi	taxi
tamponi	tampons
tanek(-nka/-o)	thin
tat(-ica)	thief
tatarska omaka	tartar sauce
teden	week
tedenski(-ska/-o)	weekly
tekoče stopnice	escalator
telečja pečenka	roast veal
telefon	telephone
telefonist	operator *(telephone)*
telefonska kabina	telephone box
telefonska kartica	phonecard
telefonski klic	telephone call
telefonski imenik	telephone directory
telesna straža	lifeguard
teletina	veal
televizija	television
telovadni copati	gym shoes
temen(-mna/-o)	dark
temno moder(-dra/-o)	navy blue
temperatura	temperature
tenis	tennis
teniška žogica	tennis ball
teniški igrišče	tennis court
terasa	terrace
termalno kopališče	thermal bathing pool

termalni izviri	thermal springs
termometer	thermometer
testenine	pasta
teža	weight
težek(-žka/-o)	hard ; heavy ; difficult
ti	you ; see GRAMMAR
tih(-a/-o)	quiet
tisti	that (one)
tlačilka za kolo	pump (bicycle)
toaletni papir	toilet paper
tolar	*Slovene unit of currency*
tolmač	interpreter
tolmin	hard sheep's-milk cheese
tonik	tonic water
topel(-pla/-o)	warm
toplice	spa
torba	bag
torek	Tuesday
torta	cake
tovarna	factory
tovornjak	lorry
trafika	tobacconist's
trajekt	car ferry
tramvaj	tram
trčenje	crash (car)
trd(-a/-o)	hard
trdo kuhano jajce	hard-boiled egg
trdnjava	fortress
trebuh	stomach
tretji(-a/-e)	third
trezor	safe
trg	square (in town)

trgovec(-ica)	shop assistant
trgovina	shop
tržnica	market
tudi	also
tuj(-a/-e)	foreign ; strange
tukaj	here
tun	tuna
tunel	tunnel
tura	tour
turist	tourist
turistična agencija	tourist office
turistična cesta	tourist road
turistična karta	tourist map
turistična vozovnica	tourist ticket
turistični kraj	tourist resort
tuš	shower

učitelj(-ica)	teacher
učiti	to teach
udoben(-bna/-o)	comfortable
ugasniti	to switch off
uhani	earrings
uleči se	to lie down
ulica	street
uloviti	to catch
umešana jajca	scrambled eggs
umetno zobovje	dentures
umetnostna galerija	art gallery
umiti (se)	to wash (oneself)
umivalnik	washbasin

univerza	university
upokojenec	pensioner
ura	watch ; hour ; clock
urad	office ; desk
usnje	leather
uspavalna tableta	sleeping pill
usta	mouth
ustaviti	to stop
utoniti	to drown
utrujen(-a/-o)	tired
v	in ; into
vaba	bait *(for fishing)*
vagon	carriage *(train)*
varen(-rna/-o)	safe
varovalka	fuse
varuška	baby-sitter
vas	village
vata	cotton wool
vaza	vase
včeraj	yesterday
več	more
večer	evening
večerja	evening meal
večji(-čja/-e)	bigger ; major
veder(-dra/-o)	happy ; cheerful
vedeti	to know
vedno	always
vedro	bucket
vegetarijanec	vegetarian

veleblagovnica	department store
veleposlalništvo	embassy
velik(-a/-o)	large ; big
velika noč	Easter
veliko	several ; many ; a lot
veljaven(-vna/-o)	valid
velur	velvet
velurno usnje	suede
veriga	chain
verjetno	probably
ves(vsa/vso)	whole ; all ; total
vesel(-a/-o)	happy
veslaški center	rowing centre
veslo	oar
veter	wind
vetrobransko steklo	windscreen
veza	connection *(train, etc)*
vezati	to connect
vi	you ; see GRAMMAR
video kamera	camcorder
video	video
videti	to see
vidio kaseta	video tape
vidva	you two ; see GRAMMAR
vijak	screw
vijoličast(-a/-o)	purple
vilica	fork *(for eating)*
vino	wine
vinograd	vineyard
vinska cesta	wine route
vinska karta	wine list
višina	height

visok krvni pritisk	**high blood pressure**
visok(-a/-o)	**tall**
vitamin	**vitamin**
viza	**visa**
vizitka	**card**
vklopiti	**to switch on**
vlak	**train**
vlažen(-žna/-o)	**damp**
vleči	**to tow**
vključen(-čna/-o)	**included**
vnet(-a/-o)	**sore**
vnetje	**infection**
voda	**water**
vodič	**guidebook**
vodja	**leader**
volnen(-a/-o)	**woollen**
vodnik	**guide**
vogal	**corner**
vohati	**to smell**
vojna	**war**
volna	**wool**
voltaža	**voltage**
vonj	**smell**
voz	**carriage** (railway)
voziček	**trolley**
voziček za prtljago	**luggage trolley**
voziti	**to drive**
vozni red	**timetable** (transport)
voznik	**driver**
vozniško dovoljenje	**driving licence**
vozovnica	**fare** (train, bus, etc)
vprašati	**to ask**

vrat	neck
vrata	door ; gate
vratar	porter *(for door)*
vrč	jug ; jar
vrednostni predmeti	valuables
vreme	weather
vremenska napoved	weather forecast
vreti	to boil
vrh	top ; summit
vrniti	to return
vroč(-a/-e)	hot
vročina	heat ; fever
vrsta	queue
vrt	garden
vrv	rope
vrvica	string
vsak	every
vsak dan	every day
vsakdo	everyone
vse (vsa/vso)	every(thing)
vsebovati	to contain
vsota	amount
vstati	to get up *(out of bed)*
vstop	entrance
vstopnica	entrance ticket
vstopnina	entrance fee
vtičnica	socket *(electrical)*
vtikač	electric plug
vzeti	to take
vzhod	east
vžig	ignition
vžigalnik	lighter

z	with
za	for
zabava	party (celebration)
zabavati se	enjoy oneself
začasno	temporary
začetek	start
začeti	to begin
začimbe za solato	salad dressing
začinjenje	dressing (for food)
zadaj	behind
zadnji(-a/-e)	last
zadrga	zip
zahod	west
zajec	rabbit
zajtrk	breakfast
zajtrkovalnica	breakfast room
zakaj?	why?
zakonska postelja	double bed
zamašek	plug
zamenjati	to change
zamuda	delay
zamuditi	to miss (plane, train, etc)
zanimiv(-a/-o)	interesting
zanimiv objekt	site of special interest
zapestnica	bracelet
zapisek	note
zapreti	to close
zaprto	closed
zarja	dawn
zaročen(-a)	engaged (to be married)
zaročenec	fiancé
zaročenka	fiancée

zaščitna čelada	crash helmet
zaseden(-a/-o)	engaged *(phone, toilet, etc)* ; full
zastava	flag
zastoj v prometu	hold-up *(traffic)*
zastrupitev s hrano	food poisoning
zavarovanje	insurance
zavesa	curtain
zavitek	package
zaviti	to wrap (up)
zavore	brakes
zavrteti številko	to dial *(telephone)*
zbirati	to collect
zdravilo proti bolečinam	painkiller
zdravilo	drug ; medicine
zdravnik	doctor
Združene države Amerike	United States of America
zelen(-a/-o)	green
zelena karta	green card *(car insurance)*
zelena	celery
zelena solata	lettuce
zelenjava	vegetables
zelišče	herb
zelje	cabbage
zelo	very
zemljevid	detailed map
zgodaj	early
zgodovinski	historical
zgodovinski spomenik	historical monument
zgoraj	upstairs
zgradba	building
zima	winter
zimsko športno središče	winter sports centre

zimska zapora	road closed in winter
zjutraj	in the morning
zlato	gold
zlomljen(-a/-o)	broken
zmenek	appointment
zmrznjen(-a/-o)	frozen
zmrzovalnik	freezer
znak	sign ; notice
znamka	brand (make) ; stamp
znižanje	reduction
zob	tooth
zobje	teeth
zobna ščetka	toothbrush
zobna pasta	toothpaste
zobobol	toothache
zobozdravnik(-nica)	dentist
zraven	next to ; beside
zrezek	steak ; chop
zrezek na žaru	grilled steak
zunaj	outdoor
zvečer	in the evening
zveza	contact
zvonec	bell (door)
žal mi je	I'm sorry!
žaluzija	blind (for window)
žarnica	light bulb
žebelj	nail (metal)
žele	jelly
železniška blagajna	booking office (train)

železniška postaja	**railway station**
želodec	**stomach**
žemlja	**bread roll**
žena	**wife**
ženska	**woman**
ŽENSKE	**Ladies'** *(toilet)*
žepna svetilka	**torch**
žepni nož	**penknife**
žeton	**token** *(for bus, phone)*
žganje	**brandy**
žilav(-a/-o)	**tough**
živalski vrt	**zoo**
živeti	**to live**
živio!	**hello!**
življenje	**life**
življensko zavarovanje	**life insurance**
žlica	**spoon**
žlička	**teaspoon**
žlikrofi	**ravioli**
žoga	**ball**